GRATITUDE INFUSION

Workplace Strategies for a
Thriving Organizational Culture

BY

KERRY ALISON WEKELO

ISBN 10: Paperback 1-937985-45-8
ISBN 13: Paperback 978-1-937985-45-5
ISBN 10: Hardcover 1-937985-43-1
ISBN 13: Hardcover 978-1-937985-43-1
eISBN 10: 1-937985-46-6
eISBN 13: 978-1-937985-46-2

Printed in the United States of America

TABLE OF CONTENTS

Introduction 1

Chapter 1   Why Gratitude 4

Chapter 2   Gratitude Beginnings................................. 10

Chapter 3   The Research on Gratitude 16

Chapter 4   Life Lessons on Gratitude......................... 22

Chapter 5   Practice and Communicate Gratitude 29

Chapter 6   Receive Gratitude...................................... 47

Chapter 7   Handle Challenges with Gratitude........... 53

Chapter 8   Award with Gratitude 64

Chapter 9   Give Back... 74

Chapter 10   Gratitude in Uncertain Times 90

Chapter 11   Grateful Companies in Action................. 96

Chapter 12   Conclusion 126

Chapter 13   Outward Gratitude....................................128

Notes..130

INTRODUCTION

In 2017, I launched my book and program, *Culture Infusion*. This was a case study of Actualize Consulting's internal journey to revamp our culture. While Actualize has been financially successful since its inception in 2003, its internal company culture needed some developing. Our early years were fraught with high attrition, conflict, and unhappy employees. In 2010, I read a book called *Leadership and Self-Deception: Getting Out of the Box* by the Arbinger Institute. It explained the importance of taking accountability and aligning your goals.

Feeling inspired, I brought this book to the partners. We agreed that we needed to step up and set our priorities together in order to solve the problems we were facing. It was then that we decided to focus on our people... *first*. We started infusing leadership operations with the same techniques I found successful in my personal life, like a focus on effective communication, personal wellness, healthy work/life balance, solving conflict, encouraging team connection, setting intentions, and more. Once leadership was applying these principles, we were able to expand them to our employees and the process of infusing our culture was on its way. Six years after we decided to put our people first, our attrition rates that were once at 33% dropped to less than 1%. We are currently enjoying a low 4% turnover rate for the last four years and we are proud to have been named *Top Company Culture* by *Entrepreneur Magazine*, a *Top Workplace* by *The Washington Post*, and *Great Place to Work-Certified*. The average tenure is five years with 14% of our people staying over ten years.

These impressive results did not go unnoticed by clients. They saw our employees happy to show up to work, putting extensive effort into doing their job well, and excited to do it all again the next day. They would ask us what we were doing to make it this way, and the answer was simple; we were focusing on our people. But when it comes to putting that into practice, it isn't as straight-forward. So, I turned our people-centric approach into 9 principles that could be implemented with any team. Each principle contains actionable tips, exercises, and examples of how they can be integrated into any team or leadership style. We decided to turn it into a service offering, and *Culture Infusion* was born.

It picked up from there. Clients were happy; I began getting requests to do segments from major news sources like ABC and NPR. Attrition rates are a very expensive problem for companies, and the ten-fold success of seeing people improving their operations with tips and guided navigation from our own firm's growing pains was humbling. But more importantly, hearing how our clients' *employees* were happier because of my tips was so rewarding. It reinforced my passion for helping others and my knack for problem solving. I enjoy creating tailored solutions for others because I know that one size does not fit all.

In the years since its release, the 9 guiding principles of the *Culture Infusion* program remain largely the same. The one thing missing, however, was a foundation of gratitude. Now, in 2020, on the 10th anniversary of our decision to focus on our people, *Gratitude Infusion* is taking the stage. This book can be seen as a supplement to *Culture Infusion*, but the wealth of information inside stands alone. Each of these chapters offer perspective and a dash of creativity to inspire your team and leadership through the lens of gratitude. Whether you are giving an award, working through conflict, or striving to reinvigorate your team, gratitude is always the answer.

I am grateful for the success of *Culture Infusion*, the support of my clients and team, and that people have seen results from my tips. One of my favorite honors was a client who told me that my work was "purposeful, positive, and proactive." They told me that my "influence on making the world a better place has grown exponentially, at a time when it is more important than ever." I always strive to provide tips that are easy to implement, create positive change, and have meaning behind them. And the idea that I make the world a better place simply because I am living life to the best of my ability and sharing my passion is very flattering. I share these tips because living them makes my world a better place. They are not just a set of instructions, but a lifestyle.

I hope you enjoy reading how gratitude has changed my life, my relationships, my leadership style, and my perspective. I truly think you will find that the ripple effect from even the smallest wave of gratitude is quite large.

CHAPTER 1
Why Gratitude

Gratitude is extremely easy to practice. It's effective. It's quick. It's free. You can practice it anytime, anyplace, anywhere, for anything. Finding aspects of your life for which to be grateful can shift your energy to focus on the positives when faced with adversity.

Gratitude is the most powerful tool I have ever used; it never fails to lift the spirits of all involved. In fact, I believe it's so powerful that we must infuse gratitude into all aspects of our lives. My grandmother Greco taught me that a good cook layers the flavors. If you season the meal along the way, she'd say, the food will be infused with a richer flavor. It's the same with our lives. Infusing gratitude into every opportunity that arises results in much richer lives—your own and those around you.

It might seem natural to show gratitude to family or other areas of your personal life, and a bit more complex to focus on gratitude in your workplace. That's where *Gratitude Infusion* comes in. This book will give you workplace strategies using gratitude to build and boost an organizational culture. Through gratitude you can show people the positive impact they're having and why that impact is important to the organization. It's a powerful way to infuse your culture with goodwill, positivity, and the best of humanity.

At Actualize Consulting, where I serve as Chief Operating Officer, we make gratitude a daily practice. This simple practice quickly made the company a more purposeful and more meaningful place to work.

On the inside cover page of this book, you will see a Gratitude Bubble where you can fill in the things you choose to welcome into your personal space. We can decide and define who and what we let into our personal bubbles. Personally, I choose to no longer let news-watching into my bubble. I find that social media feeds and conversations with others keep me adequately in the loop on current events while protecting my energy from the negative vibes I used to experience from watching the news. Even if the news is on in a doctor's office or restaurant, I try to not focus on the screen. I also choose my friends more wisely; I take a moment before saying yes to commitments. And I make gratitude the forefront of my Gratitude Bubble. Gratitude is my protector and shield against negativity and struggle.

I was inspired to design the illustration to incorporate many languages because gratitude is universal. It brings us all together no matter where each of us is from. A wise soul told me, "No matter the language gratitude is given in, it's always understood, appreciated, and never forgotten."

Professionally, I choose to lead with gratitude and to express my gratitude as often as I feel inspired to share it. One exercise that I facilitate in my seminars, called *Spread Gratitude Outward*, is a particularly strong testament to the power of gratitude. The exercise invites each participant to spend two minutes freely sharing with a partner what they are grateful for, without interruption. This allows participants to experience how easily we can change our perspective and find things in our world to be grateful for. The speed and depth of the mood change in the room has often mesmerized me as the group energy shifts to joy and elation. At the end of the session, I challenge the participants to keep the flow of gratitude moving by expressing gratitude verbally or in a written letter to a team member or someone in their personal life.

Such examples of the energetic shifts that gratitude incites are countless. In this book, the focus will be on sharing real stories of gratitude and how those stories can be applied both personally and in the workplace to create a thriving organizational culture. I include the personal element because gratitude pays no attention to the human boundaries of our personal and work lives; it flows like water whenever and wherever it can.

The gratitude ripple effect is powerful. Creating a thriving culture of gratitude positively impacts everyone who touches that culture—individuals, teams, managers, and, ultimately, clients. Gratitude allows our teams to bond and work together from a place of positivity. By having a standardized method of communication that incorporates gratitude, we save time and minimize conflict. Our people experience less stress when they practice gratitude, which, in turn, results in better health. And managers that lead from a place of gratitude are more fulfilled.

Structure of This Book

To lead by example, we must personally practice whatever it is that we want others to do. Thus, **Chapter 2** begins with a condensed version of my personal and professional journey with gratitude—the key lessons learned from those experiences and how those lessons have shaped my teaching and leading, both personally and professionally.

Chapters 3 and 4 follow with the research and life lessons of gratitude, respectively.

Chapters 5–10 cover strategies for instituting gratitude to create a thriving organizational culture: practicing and communicating gratitude, receiving gratitude, handling challenges with gratitude, awarding with gratitude, giving back, and employing gratitude through uncertain times.

Chapter 11 provides inspiring case studies of individuals who share practical examples of the power of gratitude in their own lives and organizations.

Chapter 12 offers a concluding summary of the book. The final chapter, **Chapter 13,** fittingly sends gratitude outward to those who collaborated in creating this book.

How to Use This Book

This book is for anyone who wants to add more gratitude to their lives, personally and professionally. Most of the practices in this book are suitable for both individuals and groups. And all of the strategies offered are *free*. They simply require your time, attention, and commitment to focus on gratitude in all areas of life.

The workplace strategies for a thriving organizational culture presented in **Chapters 5–10** build on each other, so I recommend you read them in order. However, if you need some ideas and recommendations about a particular strategy, feel free to skip around;

you will still get plenty of usable information and you can always revisit a previous chapter at a later time.

Take your time with each section, allowing your ideas to formulate about how you can incorporate this new approach into your personal and corporate life. Answer the questions throughout the book and do the exercises in the Gratitude-Expanding Experience section at the end of each chapter. These exercises will both solidify and expand your learning. Whether you decide to handwrite your thoughts in a journal or type them on your computer or other device, take the time to go inward. That's where we learn—from our inner wisdom.

GRATITUDE-EXPANDING EXPERIENCE

How do you prefer to document your learning and reflections? Before you start this book, determine how you will do this; for instance, will you write your thoughts in a new notebook or type them on a computer?[1]

"Gratitude
works because
**you can't be grateful
and negative
at the same time;**
it counteracts feelings of envy,
anger, greed, and other states
harmful to happiness."

Leading
researcher and psychologist,
Robert A. Emmons,
from his book,
Gratitude Works!

CHAPTER 2

Gratitude Beginnings

I could write an entire book on personal stories of how gratitude has guided me seamlessly through life. Below, I share some of the key stories that shape who I am today and that have given me the power to see the brighter side of things. Through these experiences, I began to choose to see gratitude in each moment.

Childhood

As a child, I used to play a game to try to get people to smile or pivot to being happy when upset or angry. It started with my maternal grandmother, whom I loved dearly. My brother and I spent a vast amount of time with her as my single mom worked. She was a bit of a firecracker in her day and did not want to be called Grandma, so we called her Gloria.

Gloria was not overly happy about babysitting us, so we were constantly on high alert about our behavior. No matter how well behaved I was, however, I seemed to always displease her in some way. So one day I decided to play a game in which I would be grateful for all that was around me, especially the beauty of my surroundings. I vividly remember the farmland filled with cows and chickens, a river to explore, and a sky of stars at night. There was always something positive to which I could pivot.

Then I expanded the game to my grandmother. Trying to get her to pivot and smile, I would be silly, give her compliments, praise her in words of gratitude for watching over us. If I could shift her energy in the slightest way, such as evoking a smile or bringing out her playful side, I considered it a win.

To this day, I am grateful for this game; even now, it helps me deal with challenging conversations easily.

High School/College

One of my best friends from high school had cancer. Over the course of our relationship she cycled in and out of the hospital. As her disease progressed, she barely attended school. She had been fighting for over ten years before passing away. Her zest for seeing the good in everything and being grateful for a day when we could play was life-changing for me. When you are sick like my friend was, you are thankful for one good day; one moment of feeling well enough to venture outside your home.

After my friend passed, as I was helping her mom clean up her space, I found a small piece of paper with her handwritten words: "Suck it up and keep moving."

I am grateful for each moment I shared with my friend. Grateful she showed me how a little gratitude could shift one's perspective. She rarely complained and was always grateful for the smallest things: her dog's companionship, the latest Pearl Jam song, going to the movies, or eating Sour Patch Kids candy. Her legacy lives on in a children's activity book I wrote and dedicated in her memory,

Wonders of Your Mind.[3] I donate the book's proceeds to less fortunate kids, and I know she is smiling from above.

Divorce

When I decided to get a divorce, I determined to focus on gratitude, the positives of our family, and the solid relationship we had developed with my children's dad. At first, he was not on board with the gratitude focus, yet I remained relentless in my quest for peace for our family and kids, just as I had previously with my grandmother Gloria.

As I focused on our strength of seamlessly working together as a team, the new normal began working well. It continues to work because we both are exceptionally organized and willing to assist each other as needed; rather than sticking to a rigid schedule of who has the kids, we flow as our schedules and their schedules dictate. For example, if one of us needs to be out of town, the other steps up, no questions.

Our kids' friends' parents who see us at sporting events many times do not even know we are divorced. When they find out, they say, "You have a better relationship than most married couples."

I also host Thanksgiving every year, and his family still joins us. I even invite his family to our annual beach vacation.

Gratitude has enabled us to provide a loving environment for our kids.

Challenges

One of the strategies I use when facing a conflict or challenge is my **3P Method of Pausing to Pivot to a Positive**. Instead of spending too much time focused on the negative, I now quickly pivot to a positive possibility or lesson learned. Here is an overview of how it works:

1. **Pause.** Take a breath and pause to listen to each other. By taking a moment, you give yourself and the other person space to think before reacting. Think of why you are grateful in this moment. This helps to diffuse negative emotions and tension and focus your energy on gratitude.

2. **Pivot.** Now you are in a space to pivot to the positive. Pivot out of the angry or negative or blaming cycle. Try to think of things from a third-person point of view. This can help you gain a better understanding of the situation at hand.

3. **Positive Possibilities.** Become allies as you work together to explore a variety of positive possibilities and outcomes for the situation. Shared resolution of the issue helps you to move forward together. This will help eliminate any residual negative feelings.

Applying the 3P Method has brought more peace and calm into my household and workplace. As I continue to evolve, I have expanded the 3P Method to include gratitude, which I will discuss more in Chapter 7: Handle Challenges with Gratitude.

Seminars

As I mentioned in the first chapter, using gratitude in my seminars has been a gamechanger for how people respond to the information I am providing. The beautiful thing about the topic of gratitude is that I can use it in any of my seminars because it always works! One participant who messaged me after the *Spread Gratitude Outward* exercise shared that he had been having conflict with one of his team members. After my seminar, he had coffee with the individual and led the conversation with gratitude. Noting that everything shifted in their relationship at that point, he mentioned how easy it was to share words of gratitude with that team member and that the effectiveness was mind-boggling for him. He agreed to continue to lead with gratitude by expressing it more regularly and in the moment with his team.

These stories of gratitude and daily grateful moments remind me that I can lift myself up from any negative situation if I focus on gratitude. It takes practice and patience, but I promise you that the results are well worth the effort.

GRATITUDE-EXPANDING EXPERIENCE

What is one of your fondest memories of feeling content?

What were you grateful for in this memory?

Write about why it was impactful and any lessons you learned.

My books mentioned in the previous sections:

CHAPTER 3

The Research on Gratitude

Many people are drawn to facts, figures, science, and proof in research. I prefer to feel things out, follow my intuition, and live in the moment. But that does not work for everyone.

I taught a seminar on stress management based on my six daily principles[4] that have worked for me, my clients, and my team members for over nine years. These principles are to focus on movement, breathing, handling challenges, nourishment, communicating, and doing an activity you love each day. To me, feeling better was proof of the principles' effectiveness and importance.

However, one participant stated in her review survey: "I am a scientist; I need to know the facts on why I need to reduce stress." I had just assumed that we all know it is beneficial to reduce stress, hence the seminar on stress management. For days, I struggled with the constructive feedback, until one of my coaches reminded me that all the other feedback was positive and our tendency is to focus on the one piece that is giving us true feedback. I stayed grounded in the positive feedback I received and quickly pivoted to gratitude for seeing another's perspective. I realized that not everyone is a natural believer that feeling good feels better.

I was pretty sure I knew who had made the comment; it was a woman who had seemed hesitant about the techniques taught throughout the class. Fast forward to the following year where I was teaching another seminar on stress management. When the same participant walked in, I said, "Hi, so nice to see you again."

"Do I know you?" she asked.

She had no recollection of being in my seminar the previous year, yet she had left an impact on me. In fact, she is the reason I added tons of data to my lesson on the science of positive thinking and gratitude and why these practices help reduce stress. I was so excited to share my research with her and the others. After the class when the surveys came back, one person—who I am confident was the same participant—stated that, again, there was not enough data. This time I did not let her comment have the same concerning impact. I was able to stand in gratitude as I do believe my stress management seminar is much more powerful with the data backing each point and exercise.

Research from Gratitude Experts

Gratitude has immense benefits. According to neuroscientist Glenn Fox, "Gratitude relies on the brain networks associated with social bonding and stress relief; this may explain in part how grateful feelings lead to health benefits over time. Feeling grateful and recognizing help from others creates a more relaxed body state and allows the subsequent benefits of lowered stress to wash over us."[5] To find out exactly what those benefits are, I will share research on gratitude from several experts to support the ideas in this book and my encouragement to adopt gratitude as a way of life.

Robert A. Emmons

Robert A. Emmons is the leading psychologist in research and books on gratitude. To prepare for writing this book, I purchased all of his writings. I love psychology, so I was especially drawn to his book *The Psychology of Gratitude*.[6] The book is dense and comprehensive, with a description that states: "Gratitude, like other positive emotions, has inspired many theological and philosophical writings, but it has inspired very little vigorous, empirical research." I was pleased to witness Emmons's efforts to "prove" that gratitude is positive.

One of my favorite parts of his book is the summary of the scientific results of his research. "Gratitude," Emmons states, "is related to 23 percent lower levels of stress hormones. Dietary fat intake is reduced by as much as 25 percent when people keep a gratitude journal, and gratitude is related to a 10 percent improvement in sleep quality in patients with chronic pain."

Emmons summarizes: "The effects of gratitude are not limited to the physical realm. Just to give a glimpse into its benefits, gratitude increases self-esteem, enhances willpower, strengthens relationships, deepens spirituality, boosts creativity, and improves academic performance. Given the range of these positive outcomes, gratitude has fittingly been referred to as the quintessential positive trait, the amplifier of goodness in oneself, the world, and others, and having unique ability to heal, energize, and change lives."

We know we feel better when we practice gratitude, yet having the research is helpful for understanding why it's key to us personally and professionally.

Adrian Gostick and Chester Elton

Best-selling authors and cofounders of The Culture Works, a global training company, Adrian Gostick and Chester Elton have dedicated their work to improving corporate culture. In fact, they wrote an entire book on the importance of leading with gratitude, called just that: *Leading with Gratitude*. Quoting statistics from the US Department of Labor, they point out, "The number one reason people give on third-party exit interviews is they don't feel appreciated by their manager for their specific contributions."[7] They go on to say, "It's no shock, then, to learn that our research shows frequent, genuine gratitude at work has been correlated with up to 50 percent lower employee turnover." I completely agree with this sentiment – I believe that a large portion of our low turnover rates at Actualize are due to our gratitude focus.

Brené Brown

Brené Brown has inspired me personally with her unique ability to research data and reveal it via riveting storytelling. If you have not seen her speak, I recommend taking some time to watch her videos; she's captivating. One of my favorites is her Netflix special *Brené Brown: The Call to Courage*.[8] In it, Brown talks about her research on gratitude and how she incorporates gratitude with her family. She tells a story of her daughter and boyfriend going off to a party together. Fearful of their safety as teenagers traversing new territory of responsibility, she kept saying over and over why she was grateful for them. She then proceeded to talk about how people who have experienced life-altering events, such as death or loss of job or house, have turned to gratitude as a cure.

I searched for the facts to support her talk. In an article written for the Global Leadership Network, Brown states, "In my 12 years of research on 11,000 pieces of data, I did not interview one person who had described themselves as joyful, who also did not actively practice gratitude."[9] She goes on to say, "For me it was very counterintuitive because I went into the research thinking that the relationship between joy and gratitude was: if you are joyful, you should be grateful. But it wasn't that way at all. Instead, practicing gratitude invites joy into our lives."

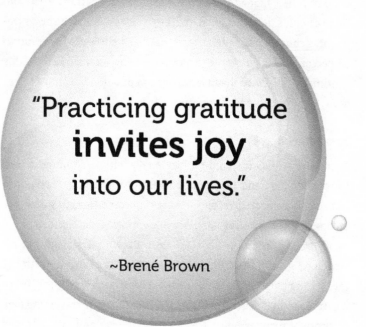

"Practicing gratitude **invites joy** into our lives."

~Brené Brown

GRATITUDE-EXPANDING EXPERIENCE

Do you believe that gratitude could help shift your perspective? Take a moment to ponder your answer and explain why. To practice how gratitude feels, take a moment to list 10 items you are grateful for at this very moment. The things you list can be big or small; for example, maybe you just got a promotion or are simply grateful that you have shelter.

CHAPTER 4

Life Lessons on Gratitude

I have a cabinet full of cards and stationery I have collected because I have always loved expressing myself through the written word and sharing in gratitude with others. The act of putting pen to paper stimulates part of my brain in a way that is as comforting as a soft plush sweater on a cold, dreary day.

A few years ago, a desire to write arose in me, and I started dabbling in a few gratitude letters to my closest friends and family. The turning point was writing a letter to my grandmother Greco, pleading with her to move closer so she could have the support of family in her last chapter of life. I had visions of learning more of her famous recipes, spending holidays together, and just having my kids get to know her better. I hoped that if I poured my heart into the words and offered to help, she would accept the invitation.

My grandmother respectfully wrote back saying no. At first, my heart felt heavy and sad, yet I realized that at least I had revealed my true feelings. I politely wrote back letting her know I understood and offered an open invitation.

Communicating via written letter instead of phone, email, or text, I felt as if I were in the olden days, and the urge to keep writing spurred me on—what other feelings would be uncovered?

Trusting my gut, I decided to write letters to friends, relatives, and business associates. I set no parameters or expectations; my goal was simply to use the beautiful stationery and cards I had accumulated over the years.

I wrote my sentiments as if they were my last words to each person, deliberately expressing myself from a place of gratitude and appreciation. A sense of contentment embodied me fully as the words formed. I felt liberated. I had finally told my family how much I love them and my favorite coach how much he had touched my life.

Yet, I also felt something unsettling. When I called one of my mentors to talk about my inner restlessness, she gracefully reminded me that I had yet to write about the other emotions—the anger and grief that had been bottled up and neatly stored in the depths of my soul.

For those last letters, I let go of the neat handwriting and fine presentation. My sloppy handwriting matched the scrap paper as I released yucky trapped emotions and old resentments. Those letters I did not mail; I burned them.

```
 dissapproval
  aggressiveness
submission
        love
  optimism
```

Finally, the spectrum of emotions that we all experience had revealed itself to me, making each emotion fuller as I felt the contrasts between them. In feeling pain, for example, I knew a greater depth of joy.

Allowing ourselves to experience these contrasts makes our lives richer, but if we're not paying attention, we can let ourselves slide downward into our issues. Practicing gratitude can help us climb back up. I have dealt with some difficult issues in my life, as we all have in our journeys, but I always turn to gratitude and it works beautifully.

Before we explore how to cultivate a practice of gratitude in the next chapter, let's take a brief look at the spectrum of emotions. We must be able to feel and recognize all of them to pivot to gratitude and heal any hurt.

Spectrum of Emotions

Love (serenity, joy, ecstasy)

Love has always been present in many forms. Many times, we are too blinded by our other emotions to see who truly loves us.

I was formed by the love of the adult figures surrounding me as they showed me the variety of ways that love can be expressed. I truly know there is more than one way to deal with the things in front of us, yet I know if we choose love, the world opens up. This was an important lesson to learn.

Submission (acceptance, trust, admiration)

I may have a wild and crazy family, but don't we all? We all have pain and suffering from our childhood. I realized that even though times were crazy, I could find valuable lessons, knowledge, and perseverance in the midst of things.

My family is one of the most accepting families I have experienced. Even if someone gets divorced, for instance, we still consider the partner to be family. We are always there for each other, even if we are fighting along the way. That is life and part of the emotional spectrum.

And then there were the life lessons I learned from my grandmother Gloria, who was both strong and stern. Once I forgave all the hurtful comments sent my way of not being good enough or skinny enough, I saw that she taught me to roll up my sleeves and not be afraid to get dirty, figuratively and literally. She never held back, and there was never a question of what was on her mind. That kind of honesty builds a resounding sense of trust.

Disapproval (pensiveness, sadness, grief)

Toward the end of my letter-writing journey, I was confused and sad. After writing letters to my ex-husband and brother, I cried for a good hour. I had always been putting on a happy face—seeing only the good. I had not allowed myself to feel the other more difficult emotions. I had not fully processed the pain of rejection in my marriage or the lack of a childhood.

I had never allowed myself to be sad or acknowledge that at the age of five, I decided not to be a burden to my single mom but instead to be her helper and my brother's stable rock. I see now that nobody asked that of me; I had made the decision myself. All my life I had been the caregiver. Once I saw that, I was sad that I rarely allowed anyone to care for me. My catchphrase had always been, "I will take care of it."

The lesson here is that it is okay to be sad, grieve, and ask for help along the way; it is a necessary part of everyone's process.

Aggressiveness (annoyance, anger, rage)

These emotions are the ones that we tend to store because we don't want to upset anyone or express how we are truly feeling. I had told many a friend or client to write about these emotions and then burn those writings for release. Yet, I had not done this exercise for myself.

In the letter-writing exercise I mentioned earlier, I was able to, in a not-so-subtle way, express aggressive feelings about things that had pissed me off in my life. The best release was a letter to my first stepdad. I've always experienced him as a big jerk who's made my life miserable on many occasions. As I wrote, I allowed myself not to see a positive side of him; he may have one, but it has never been revealed to me. And that is finally acceptable. In writing that letter, I gave myself the compassionate gift of a safe space to speak the truth of what I had experienced.

The lesson here is that sometimes letting go of hurt is the only solution. Even if there is no true closure or apology.

Optimism (interest, anticipation, vigilance)

The emotional spectrum comes full circle with the realization that we must go through the good, the bad, and the ugly for true healing to occur. I am overjoyed with excitement for what the future will hold. I have confidence to allow all emotions to flow through me as I experience their energy instead of bottling up the negative thoughts. The lesson of optimism is that you view the world how you choose to see it. Here is a poem that I find explains this very well.

On Pain[10]

Your pain is the breaking of the shell that encloses your understanding. Even as the stone of the fruit must break, that its heart may stand in the sun, so must you know pain.

And could you keep your heart in wonder at the daily miracles of your life, your pain would not seem less wondrous than your joy.

And you would accept the seasons of your heart, even as you have always accepted the seasons that pass over your fields.

And you would watch with serenity through the winters of your grief.

Much of your pain is self-chosen. It is the bitter potion by which the physician within you heals your sick self.

Therefore trust the physician and drink his remedy in silence and tranquility.

For his hand, though heavy and hard, is guided by the tender hand of the Unseen.

And the cup he brings, though it burn your lips has been fashioned of the clay which the Potter has moistened with His own sacred tears.

~Kahlil Gibran

GRATITUDE-EXPANDING EXPERIENCES

Personal: In the classic film *It's a Wonderful Life*, George Bailey is shown what the world would have been like without him. He sees all the gifts he brought into the world and begins to appreciate the wonderful life he had. This is now called the George Bailey Effect. The more we recognize the kindness we receive and give, the more comes our way.

How can you start to shift your thinking to an attitude of gratitude for your life? List five ways you have impacted others positively.

Workplace: Can you remember a time you used gratitude with your teams? What was the outcome?

Gratitude Infusion: How is gratitude used at a corporate level in your organization? What is your vision of adding gratitude as a firm-wide strategy?

CHAPTER 5
Practice and Communicate Gratitude

To truly feel the benefits of gratitude, we must cultivate an attitude of positivity and appreciation daily. As we feel the impact of gratitude shifting our perspective and allowing us to flow gracefully through challenges, we can then more readily share positivity and appreciation with our teams at work.

There are countless ways to practice gratitude. As Dr. Robert A. Emmons said, "You are never too old, too young, too rich, too poor, to live gratefully." Gratitude is easily accessible; it simply takes diligent practice.

Personally, I keep a gratitude journal, but I go through phases with it. I will start and stop and start again as necessary. Journaling is my go-to when I am facing a challenge. I keep a journal by my bed, and if I feel off balance or negative, I will journal on gratitude before I go to sleep.

Gratitude journaling is a very well-known practice, but there are many other ways to strengthen your gratitude muscle. My kids and I share what we are grateful for at dinner when we sit down for meals together. At Thanksgiving, my family and I write down why we are grateful on pieces of paper that we then place in a basket. Each person reads someone else's gratitude from the basket. I typically host twenty to thirty people at Thanksgiving, all of whom love the tradition.

Expressing gratitude also doesn't need to be a grand gesture; it can be as simple as telling someone that they did a job well. For example, as I was writing this book, I was conducting a seminar at a venue where the staff went out of their way to make me feel welcome and ensure I had all I needed. Before I left, I made a point to let the manager know what an amazing team they had. I told her how the gentleman leading the event had made sure the projector was working and connected to Wi-Fi to show a video. And when the others started to arrive, he welcomed everyone and ensured each person had the drink of their choice. He continued to check up on the group frequently, as if he were reading our minds. It only took a few minutes to express gratitude to this team that had made my day—and, hopefully, hearing the gratitude made their day in return.

In *The Little Book of Gratitude*,[11] Dr. Emmons provides easy suggestions to practice gratitude. My favorite is the gratitude prompts designed to get you writing in your journal. For example, think of how someone else has impacted you. Dr. Emmons suggests that instead of just saying you are grateful for a particular person, dig deeper to discuss why. Here is one of the prompts:

> "The other day, I felt really glad when ___ took the time, or made the effort to ____."

Providing examples of why you are grateful strengthens the connection you feel with your personal gratitude. As we continue this chapter, ponder how you can add more gratitude into your daily routine. Next, we will traverse how to practice gratitude in the workplace.

Remember that not everyone in your organization will immediately get on the bandwagon of gratitude. Also remember that this reluctant phase is temporary; as your teams start to feel the positive impact, their reluctance will fade. Rad Pop, Manager at Actualize Consulting, said of our gratitude-focused team building: "I at first felt like it was just another task; more work on my plate. But actually, it is a breath of fresh air that makes you look at your life from a different perspective." He continued to describe how he appreciates our focus on playfulness, gratefulness, mindfulness, and wellness at Actualize.

Rad's comment made me reflect on why I choose to keep things fresh at Actualize and continuously offer new programs and ideas: nothing is one size fits all; one activity may inspire one person, and another activity may inspire someone else. Variety is key. Below are a few suggestions of how to practice gratitude with your teams.

Start at the Beginning

When recruiting, first impressions really are everything. The candidates are not merely looking for a job; they are looking for a home. It is important that they immediately feel welcome and appreciated. Think about your current recruiting process. How do you give a potential employee a sense of your culture?

At Actualize, it is important that our recruits already feel a part of the family. We have our resident superstar, Theresa Santoro, on the front lines interviewing talent and introducing them to our company atmosphere. **Let's hear from Theresa on her strategy:**

Because gratitude is so infused into our culture at Actualize, our story does a lot of the work for us. Whenever a recruit first talks to me, one of my questions is if they are familiar with our service offerings. We are known for our financial services, but I'm always curious to know if they are aware of all the work we put into our culture. I like to educate them on our firm's history and how it was our clients that majorly inspired making Culture Infusion all that it is today.

We used to have clients ask us how our people were so upbeat and happy—and, at first, it was facetious: "So, what kind of coffee are you guys drinking at Actualize?" They were consistently seeing our consultants show up eager to get the job done, and they were genuinely curious about what we were doing to support this. Our formula is and has always been simple: happy people produce great work. The real reason our employees seem so happy is because they genuinely are.

Our main priority at Actualize is not profit; it is our employees—specifically, their goals, their career, and their well-being. We want them to have a workplace that makes them proud to show up each day, supports them, and lights them up. In my opinion, there is no way to "sell" a great workplace culture. Firms either work toward creating a thriving culture by putting their employees first, or they fall flat. No amount of marketing can salvage this or "trick" recruits.

Once you have a supportive organizational culture as your foundation, there are multiple tools available to ensure that culture extends to your recruits. For example, if a candidate has not yet made a decision on our offer, we like to check in and follow up. When we are in the interviewing process, we keep detailed notes of their interests and skill sets and make sure they talk to a wide variety of people at our firm. From day one, it is essential to us that they know they will start doing work that they are passionate about with supportive team members. The bottom line is, whether or not the recruit chooses to join your firm, you should always be grateful for their time.

Majorly, though, it is our culture that sets us apart and does the recruiting for us. Candidates know that when they join our firm, they are not just a number to us. They are a real person with feelings, aspirations, and goals, who deserves the support and care of a company that is grateful for all they have to offer. And that is our recruiting secret.

Expression of Gratitude

As mentioned above, being specific when sharing gratitude truly allows the individual to feel why you are grateful and inspires them to continue being outstanding. For example, if you say, "I am grateful for your work on the slide you put together," it may fall flat and not even be acknowledged. Instead, I use the show-and-tell approach when expressing gratitude.

For example, Craig Chapman, a Senior Manager at Actualize Consulting, put together a very descriptive slide for a presentation our Partner, Chad Wekelo, was giving at a conference. I had initially expressed gratitude but took it a step further once I received a picture of Chad at the conference with the slide in the background. I sent Craig an email titled, "You made the big screen." Then I said, "Look how awesome your slide looks! Grateful for you taking the time to pull this together. I know how busy you are with your client work."

Expressing gratitude to your teams can be done in shared corporate newsletters, handwritten letters, emails, and verbally. The key point to remember is to be specific when you share. Here are some examples from of gratitude from clients and peers.

We asked our leaders why they were grateful for the Actualize team. Here is what they had to say.

Kudos

From a client:

"You and the Actualize team have been a great pleasure to work with - **very courteous, professional, knowledgeable and dedicated -** hard to come by."

From a client:

"We have been **impressed** with the services provided by our Actualize team and **would not be where we are today without them.**"

To Brian Stitt, from Theresa Santoro, Director of HR/Operations

"Thank you for always taking on my bizarre and fun tasks at any time, and doing it with a smile emoji... **I appreciate your fun spirit,** and certainly working with you."

"I'm grateful for
the openness
of our firm that allows anyone
to express an idea or concern
freely and know
it will be heard."

~Geran Combs,
Director

"I'm grateful for
the team we have, this
pool of individuals that bring
not only strong technical skills
to the table, but also an incredible
sense of commitment and
team work. Thank you everyone
**for making this
company so
unique."**

~Priscila Nagalli,
Director

"I'm grateful for
our Actualize team because
our team makes me
better as a person
and that carries over to
my clients and what I
can offer them."

~Matt Seu, Partner

Sharing Weekly Wins

Many of us can look back at our week and easily see what we did *not* do. But when was the last time you took a moment to see what you *did* do? Our days are filled with accomplishments, or what I like to call "wins." Have you ever celebrated your wins? Take a moment to reflect on the last week. What wins did you have? How did you shine at work or help a loved one in need?

I am very hard on myself and have high internal energy that drives me to reach my goals. My coach, Catherine Hayes, suggested that each day when I make my to-do list, I also write down my daily wins. I have to admit that I do not always complete this task. I especially move away from noting my wins when I am faced with a challenging situation. But actually, a challenging day, week, or even moment is the time that the practice of writing down a list of wins is the most powerful.

Let's look at an example of how to use this practice in action. When I was faced with a key person leaving Actualize and I was feeling overwhelmed, I sent my team a list of gratitudes and wins. Reading my list, I realized that I tend to focus my gratitude outward instead of giving myself a compliment or a statement of appreciation. When we are focused outward, we are giving energy away. If we neglect to project this same positivity and gratitude inward, we can fail to lift ourselves. Self-love and generosity toward the self is an extension of the self-care I promote. Funny how a challenge made me realize I was neglecting showing gratitude for myself and yet again forgetting to focus on the wins. By revisiting this practice, I was quickly able to stabilize my mood and the situation at hand.

Gratitude Infusion

Here is an example of how to recognize personal gratitude and outward gratitude, and celebrate wins. Note that being specific is key:

- **Personal Gratitude:** My diverse skill set and resourcefulness that allows me to figure out tasks.

- **Outward Gratitude:** To Geran for his data skills to help with reporting, to Theresa for taking on the credit card reconciliation, and to Stacey for giving us more hours to support the transition.

- **Wins:** Streamlining processes as we assign tasks and provide self-service options to our team.

During this challenge I was facing, each time I felt down or defeated, I would send an email or handwritten card of gratitude to those stepping up to help. To formalize this practice, my team and I are now sharing weekly emails on our personal and outward gratitude and wins.

Ask yourself:

- **Why are you grateful for yourself?**

- **Who are you grateful for?**

- **What are your most recent wins?**

As Wayne Dyer said, "Maintain a state of gratitude and awe. Gratitude is the surest way to stop the incessant inner dialogue that leads you away from joy and perfection." And remember, you are doing the best you can today. Be gentle with yourself and focus on being grateful and the wins.

Moving with Gratitude

As one of our wellness challenges at Actualize, we included gratitude in addition to various physical activities. In my opinion, gratitude is very much related to our health and well-being. It reduces stress and makes us happier. It also brightens those around us.

We broke participants up into teams and had them compete to see who could earn the most points. You could earn points by doing something kind, participating in physical activity, cooking a healthy meal, sharing a meal with friends or co-workers, and expressing gratitude.[12] It was a healthy dose of competition and team building.

Icebreaker of Gratitude

To start or end a meeting, have the team say why they are grateful for those in the meeting. Make sure everyone is mentioned. When I facilitate this exercise, people often comment that they did not even know others were grateful for their efforts. Sharing appreciation for each other truly aids in strengthening team bonds.

Spread Gratitude Outward

As I've mentioned, sharing a flow of gratitude as a group is my favorite exercise to facilitate. I can feel the energy shift in the room as we begin focusing on gratitude.

This exercise calls for participants to pair into groups of two to each talk uninterrupted for two minutes on why they are grateful—personally and/or professionally. Participants can use a list of "I am" statements, such as "I am happy, healthy, and nourished." Or they can tell a story, perhaps even about a specific person. For inspiration, some might also choose to utilize my Zendoway Gratitude Cube.[13] No matter what they want to express, I just ask that they strive to be grateful for two minutes.

This exercise was born out of a similar one that I regularly facilitate in my seminars called *Extreme Listening*. In *Extreme Listening*, the premise is essentially the same—two minutes of uninterrupted talking with a partner whose job is to listen. However, instead of talking about gratitude, the topic is challenges. I decided to make the switch to gratitude sharing as a fun last-minute exercise one day when I had extra time at the end of a seminar. The energy shift in the room was so out of this world that I decided to include gratitude sharing as a staple exercise in my seminars.

That first day I received positive reviews from everyone in attendance, all of whom said they could feel the energy shift too. Perhaps the most powerful moment was with a gentleman who told a beautiful story about how he was grateful for time with his sister. He described how she was moving from Virginia to Texas to take care of their ailing mother and that he had been able to drive cross country with her to help her settle in. He expressed his appreciation for her putting her life on hold for their mother. He was enhanced by witnessing how hard it is to move all one's belongings and realized there was no way he would have had the strength to do what she did. With an overflowing heart, he said, "I will never *not* be grateful for her." His love and gratitude for his sister brought me to tears.

As we were leaving the meeting, the man confided, "Thank you for allowing me to express gratitude for my sister. I did not even realize how grateful I was for her until I shared with you. I am going to call her on my way home and tell her the same story."

The reason I teach is to learn from others. That day, I was touched so deeply that I now always strive to fully see the sacrifices that others make for me.

Focusing on gratitude is truly powerful and can have astounding effects.

Educating with Gratitude

Jim White, PhD, is a professor at Pensacola (FL) Christian College and is a self-described relentless networker and connector who mentors and educates business leaders of tomorrow. Jim takes his message beyond the classroom walls by inviting his students to schedule time with him to discuss the importance of LinkedIn.

Gratitude Infusion

Jim says, "I want to demonstrate to my students how critical it is to build, leverage, and promote their personal brand—and network!"

I have been tagged in dozens of photos on LinkedIn of Jim's students holding one of my cubes while standing next to all fourteen cubes arranged in a pyramid on his office shelf. I am honored that my cubes have become part of their process, so I asked Jim to explain how he utilizes Zendoway Cubes with his students. **Here's what he had to say:**

> When students come to my office, I want them to walk away having answered three questions:
>
> 1. What are your superpowers?
>
> 2. What are you passionate about?
>
> 3. How can you combine your superpowers with your passion so that you can tell your story and start branding yourself on LinkedIn?
>
> The questions take most of my students by surprise. This can be stressful as most have never thought about it. Answering requires talking about your attributes and strengths, and many are reticent to say what they are good at. The cubes have two functions during that uncomfortable moment of feeling stress and uncertainty: they calm them and open up space for self-discovery.
>
> I start by asking them to pick a cube based on a color they like. Then I read aloud a question or

prompt from the cube and hand it back to them. The cubes were designed to be squeezed like a stress ball for stress reduction and many of my students naturally begin to squeeze them.

Next, the cubes are a conversation starter and the prompts open up space for them to share.

The Gratitude Cube's open-ended prompts are a great lead-in for beginning to see what you are passionate about and what your superpowers are:

- I am grateful for...

- A strength I recently drew upon was....

- A reason I am excited for next week is...

- A highlight from today is...

- Someone that made me smile this week was...

- Something awesome I recently witnessed was...

By answering the prompts, students begin to see what gives them joy, what they are grateful for, and what they look forward to. This helps them to realize what they might want to do with their lives. One such example is a student who was pursuing her education to fulfill her parent's dream of working in their family business. During our conversation, she revealed that she was passionate about opening an orphanage in her native country.

As a college professor, my biggest joy is helping my students discover their passion, then helping them find great opportunities to put that passion to work. It is often very intense. We discuss a lot of "what ifs" and "what now?" For some students, it can be an overwhelming experience.

I use the Gratitude Cubes as a way to close the meeting and help bring the student back to the now. Again, I let the student choose the color and I choose the question. One of my favorite prompts is on the orange cube: "I am grateful for..." When I ask my students this one, I quickly get "Mom and Dad" or "family." But I push on, saying, "No, really, what are you REALLY grateful for?" With a little prodding, there is always a story: that special aunt or uncle who stood by them in dark times, a good friend helping them through a tough high school experience. My favorite story is a student raised in an orphanage in Indonesia. She had been heroically saved from extremists by the director of the orphanage. That woman changed this student's life forever. When she shared the story, she wept, even though it had happened more than a decade ago. That is gratitude.

For most, this would be where the conversation ends, but Jim does not stop there. He takes a photo of each of his students holding their Zendoway Cube and encourages them to post it on

LinkedIn. His rules of engagement are simple: find your passion, note your superpowers, share your story, and tag people. For many of these young aspiring leaders, their first post holds a smile backed by discovery and a cube in their hand. You can connect with Jim White on LinkedIn at https://www.linkedin.com/in/jimwhitepcc/.

Jim White posing with Zendoway Cubes

GRATITUDE-EXPANDING EXPERIENCES

Personal: For the next week, be explicit when expressing gratitude. For example, when my father gave me a gift card, I described the items I was going to buy, such as fuzzy slippers and a pedicure. I could have simply said, "Thank you for the gift card. I really appreciate it." But I took it a step further to say how I was going to use the gift. Be mindful and specific in your expressions of gratitude.

Workplace: What is one new way you can practice and communicate gratitude with your immediate team members? Perhaps try a weekly gratitude email exchange with your team to see how it goes. You can start with stating one reason you are grateful for each person.

Gratitude Infusion: How can you add in some of the ideas in this chapter to strengthen your firm's focus on gratitude? Who are the key players to make the effort successful?

CHAPTER 6

Receive Gratitude

Have you ever been given a compliment that was hard for you to take? For example, a friend says, "I like your shirt," and you reply, "This old thing?"

Gratitude can be hard to receive and it can take practice to receive it gracefully. For example, I have been practicing saying thank you for all compliments.

Gratitude feels good; it lifts our spirits. It heals. But we have to be mindful in receiving it. Sometimes we are so distracted with upcoming deadlines, family priorities, friends, and so on that we cannot let gratitude in.

Sometimes we are in our own personal self-doubt or unhappiness. When we don't feel good about ourselves, it is challenging to "see" when others are expressing gratitude to us. Often, we simply do not recognize it. Other times, while lingering in our own personal stories, we may struggle to accept the gift of gratitude.

Gratitude Infusion

I regularly catch myself having a hard time accepting gratitude. For example, when one of my dear friends, Melanie, gave me a bag of presents for my birthday, I was uncomfortable at first. Each gift was chosen just for me, and the amount of thought that went into each selection humbled me. Her gifts included monk fruit, a natural sugar substitute, chosen because she knows I watch my sugar intake. She also gave me a video on the teenage brain that she had once shared with her teenager and was passing on to me now that her son had flown the nest. I know that I am worthy of the lavishness of such gifts, but acceptance of that truth doesn't come easily.

As I continued going through the bag of goodies, my friend noticed my discomfort and reassured me: "Read the card. It will explain." The card expressed how I had helped her through a painful time. It said, "You saw me at my worst, but still you loved, accepted, and supported me fiercely and authentically. You saw my bright light and reminded me of my own Divine spark each time we spoke."

She was paying forward all that I have been giving to her throughout our friendship. I had never thought of it that way; I simply was being me and giving her love, gratitude, and support since those actions come naturally for me. I automatically see the best in those I come into contact with.

Kerry and Melanie

It's Human Nature

Our predisposition (or lack thereof) to gratitude is hereditary. In a study conducted by Michael Steger and colleagues, identical twins expressed more similar levels of self-reported gratitude as compared to fraternal twins. Further research by Sara Algoe suggests that the gene CD_38 has ties to gratitude. In Algoe's study, participants with this gene thanked their romantic partner 70 percent of the days of the study, while participants without the gene thanked their partner only 40 percent of the days.[14]

But whether or not you are predisposed to gratitude, you can still learn to improve your gratitude "muscle," according to Joel Wong and Joshua Brown.[15] Their 2017 study asked participants to write gratitude letters over the course of twelve weeks. At the end of the twelve-week study, gratitude had even greater effects on the participants than at the four-week mark. The more gratitude they shared, the better participants reported their overall mental health to be.

Receiving Gratitude at Work

As you are cultivating the practice of infusing gratitude into your workplace culture, it is necessary to also explore how to receive it. This encourages self-awareness and awareness of others who struggle to receive the gratitude being expressed. First, let's discuss how you can receive gratitude coming your way.

- **Self-Appreciation:** Recognize what you bring to the table. You may think, "I did what anyone would do"—just as I did in my friendship with Melanie. Give yourself credit; believe you are a good person. Recognize when you go above and beyond. Celebrate yourself!

- **See All Forms of Gratitude:** Whether it is a smile on someone's face or that small thank you they give you, take it in. Make a mental note of what you did. Write down examples of gratitude you are given daily. You may be surprised by the abundance you are receiving!

- **Validate Gratitude:** If someone does pay you gratitude, be sure to thank them instead of shrugging it off. It is a critical step in receiving. Life coach Martha Beck suggests practicing feeling the effects of this simple but profound sentence:

"Thank you; I accept."[16] Saying this sentence can be just as effective after the fact. For instance, you can hold or picture something meaningful that has already been given to you and say aloud or silently, "Thank you; I accept." Then open to the gratitude of receiving for at least several seconds.

In the workplace, instill communicating gratitude as part of your culture. Practice variety in how you express your appreciation. In the remainder of the book, there will be many examples of how to express gratitude. Before we go into those examples, keep the following in mind:

1. **Who Is the Receiver?** What form of gratitude works best for their personality? For example, one person may like to be publicly recognized while others need more daily, individual doses to keep them motivated.

2. **Remember What Works:** Turn on your radar, and tune in to the reaction of the receivers of your gratitude. Make a note of what techniques work for your individual team members. I know it seems like a lot of work, but the benefits will be immeasurable.

3. **Be Specific:** Give examples of why you are grateful. For example, with our Star Player awards (discussed in Chapter 8), we share why the winner was nominated: a recent Star Player, Jack Su, was nominated for his tenacity and creative approach to problem solving, as well as his extra effort to get the project done on time. Being specific about why you are grateful goes a very long way in making people feel appreciated and helps them realize all that they offer.

Accepting gratitude fully is something that must be cultivated and nourished. On the flip side, we have to be aware of the magnitude of our actions and be mindful in our giving. If allowing gratitude was simple, it would be more free-flowing. Even though it might not always be easy, it is important; it helps us build our self-confidence, self-awareness, and self-compassion.

GRATITUDE-EXPANDING EXPERIENCES

Personal: When was the last time you had a hard time accepting gratitude? Journal the experience and document the goodness of the giver. Write about how you are grateful for the person who recognized you. And the next time you receive the gift of gratitude, try to acknowledge it with a thank you and recognition of why you deserve what was given to you.

Workplace: List the names of your immediate team members. Using recent real-life examples, list why you are grateful for each person. Express your gratitude to each team member. Make a note of how they receive the gratitude, and pay close attention to whether they easily accept it or resist.

Gratitude Infusion: Who in your organization and life models leading with a positive and mindful mindset? What have you learned from them? Write it down and share with at least one person how they have positively impacted your life.

CHAPTER 7

Handle Challenges with Gratitude

In life, there are few things we know for certain. One of those is that we will face challenges and roadblocks—both literally and figuratively—as we navigate our daily life. We can be sailing along smoothly when BOOM, a challenge hits us out of the blue. How we navigate those challenges can make us stronger and more resilient. As the Dalai Lama said, "To remain indifferent to the challenges we face is indefensible. If the goal is noble, whether or not it is realized within our lifetime is largely irrelevant. What we must do therefore is to strive and persevere and never give up."

One of the most frequent questions I am asked is, "How do you have the capacity to do all you do?" People in my life see that I am a single mom, the COO of Actualize Consulting, and an active volunteer at school and in my community. They see that I do my best to make time for my team at work, my friends, and my family. They do not understand how I invest so much time into all these areas without feeling overwhelmed.

Gratitude Infusion

So what's my secret? I have discovered that handling challenges gracefully and as quickly as possible is the key to staying uplifted and expanding capacity. The festering, spinning, and time spent thinking about challenges are what I remember having been time consuming for me in the past. Years ago, when I was faced with a challenge, I would talk to as many people as I could that would listen. Can you relate? My contact list for discussing conflict was my mom, dad, best friend, and grandmother. One time, after spending hours venting about one particular issue, I noticed that I did not feel any better and nothing was resolved. The talking-it-out method was not working.

As Actualize Consulting started expanding and my kids participated in more activities, I had less time to spin on the challenges I was facing. I had to identify the issue at hand and move forward as quickly as possible. That is when the 3P Method of Pausing to Pivot to a Positive (described in Chapter 2) was born. This method was also a key point in my book *Culture Infusion*[17] and its chapter on handing conflict directly, openly, and immediately.

Since writing that book, I have added another crucial step to the process of handling challenges. First, I take a moment to identify my contribution to the challenge I am facing. This enables me to not place all the blame on others and to take accountability for my role. The next part of the pause is to find gratitude when facing a new challenge. I have found that gratitude and the 3P method actually go hand in hand. Use the first step, Pause, to allow all feelings, especially gratitude. Reflect on everything good in the moment to set the tone for how you can begin to problem solve.

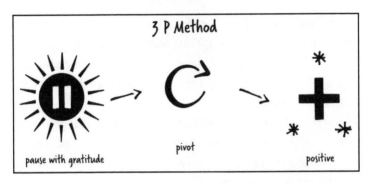

Let's explore a "before and after" using this method, with two drastically different experiences of car accidents.

Before: In 2005, when I was pregnant with my daughter, Audrey, I was rear-ended by another car. Angry, I stepped out of my car and immediately confronted the other driver. When the woman claimed she was not at fault, I started to move toward her, then suddenly stopped. We continued to argue. I called 911, and we waited. It was hot, I did not have water, and I began to panic. I started calling through my support-me phone chain. After waiting for hours for the police to arrive, I felt drained and defeated even though they agreed whoever does the rear-ending is at fault.

After: In 2019, I was on my way to a meeting with a prospective client who was in town. As I was crossing an intersection, another car collided with the side of my car. As you can imagine, I was surprised because I was simply going through a green light. Taking a deep breath, I immediately thought, *Yikes, I am going to be late for my meeting.* The lady who hit me got out of her car, screaming that I had run the red light. Taking another breath, I said, "Sorry; I know this is not what you needed today, but the light was green." I was as calm as the other woman was hysterical. I asked to exchange insurance information so we did not have to call the police. Since she would not admit to fault, I called 911. Then, instead of enlisting my phone chain, I called the prospective client and calmly explained what had happened. We decided to play it by ear about when to meet up. Next, I called my co-worker to reschedule some other meetings so I would not feel rushed. And as I waited for the police, I pivoted to gratitude: I was grateful neither of us were hurt, my client was understanding, my co-worker rescheduled my meetings, and that I could sit in my car with the heater on. Instead of arriving hours later, the police showed up within fifteen minutes. I peacefully described the incident to the officer while the lady continued to rant. The officer simply informed her, "I'm sorry, but it is clear you are at fault." I made it to my meeting about thirty minutes late without calling my go-to contact list. I paused, pivoted, and dealt with the challenge head-on by focusing on gratitude. I have to believe my newfound strategy was at play in how gracefully everything worked out.

This is just one simple example of how I deal with challenges. Another is my experience of what I now call "Brown Friday." In the midst of hosting thirty-eight people for Thanksgiving, I discovered that my toilets were not holding up. While others were shopping on Black Friday, I was trying to get a plumber to help with my situation. My family was still at my house to see the issue unfolding; my problem solving process was on full display. Instead of getting stressed or agitated, I focused on being grateful that I still had two bathrooms that worked instead of dwelling on the two that did not. I set the intention that the latter two would be fixed that day. I called two plumbers, and one said they could be out that afternoon. The plumber ended up coming within an hour and fixed everything for less than $1,000. In my book, any home repair under a $1,000 is a WIN.

By adding gratitude to the 3P Method, the short amount of time it takes to come to a resolution is mind-boggling. Even if I wanted to allow my head to spin in a challenge, it no longer feels good or productive. Plus, the impact of pausing to pivot to a positive and focusing on gratitude is cumulative. Now when I face conflict, I immediately focus on staying grateful for the things I have and can control, and the path to a resolution instantly becomes clear.

The Research on Handling Challenges with Gratitude

As you have seen, I am keen on Robert A. Emmons's research on gratitude. In his book *Gratitude Works!*[18] Emmons suggests that we remember the bad and points out how our national holiday of Thanksgiving arose from the experience of nearly half the pilgrims dying from a rough year. He summarizes in an article in *Greater Good Magazine*, "So crisis can make us more grateful—but research says gratitude also helps us cope with crisis. Consciously cultivating an attitude of gratitude builds up a sort of psychological immune system that can cushion us when we fall. There is scientific evidence that grateful people are more resilient to stress, whether minor everyday hassles or major personal upheavals. The contrast between suffering and redemption serves as the basis for one of my tips for practicing gratitude: remember the bad."[19]

Now that I have shared my personal experience and some research, let's explore handling challenges at work with gratitude.

Challenges at Work
Situational Challenges

As with my personal examples, at work I have also shifted to adding gratitude and pauses when I face conflict. I will now walk you through one of the biggest challenges I faced in my career and how gratitude was my savior.

Actualize's finance manager of thirteen years quit with only two weeks' notice. She was a key employee in our organization, and we had become dependent on her. Even though I was working to document and streamline her responsibilities, I was not at a good spot for her to leave so quickly. To amplify the stress I was already facing, accounting is my least favorite aspect of the business.

Those two weeks are a blur in my memory as I was trying to ensure we had everything covered, from paying our bills to paying our people to getting invoices out to be paid. The core of our business's financial stability was at risk, and none of those elements could wait. Everything had to continue running smoothly while I worked through the growing pains.

First, I had to deal with my own personal hurt. I had trusted our finance manager; I felt she was part of our Actualize family. I never imagined she would leave so suddenly. I was angry, I was upset, and I felt an overwhelming sense of grief and panic. I also had to analyze my part in the situation. When I decided to streamline and automate the finance function, she had said, "You cannot teach an old dog new tricks." In hindsight, if I had been more mindful about her not wanting to automate, perhaps she would have given more than two weeks' notice."

Next, as I was riding the roller coaster of emotions, I quickly pivoted to gratitude. In my gratitude pause, I reflected on the appreciation I felt toward this valuable team member. I wrote down a list:

- 13 years of dedication

- High capacity to decipher data

- Historical data records

- Allowed us to grow

- Team player who rolled up her sleeves when needed—no task was beneath her, which we needed in our small firm's operations

Each time I would return to a negative or hurt feeling, I would write down more reasons I was grateful. I sent her a gift of gratitude that consisted of three presents that I thought would be meaningful to her because of her love of horses, the beach, and shopping. I expressed my gratitude in a handwritten letter. It felt so uplifting to focus on why I was grateful instead of why I was hurt.

To this day, I am still grateful for this situation. The challenges I faced have reminded me that I am capable and ready to handle anything that comes my way. I was able to step up to help keep us soundly operating while also streamlining the finance function. I began sharing messages of gratitude and celebrating wins with my team. Even though it may have been a challenge, there were always learning experiences and small victories to celebrate.

In the midst of this transition, Theresa Santoro, our Managing Director of HR/Operations, reminded me of when we used to send out weekly gratitude as a team. She said, "I think it is time to bring that practice back." (See Chapter 5 for more detail on the practice.) Since implementing weekly gratitude, we start every week on the right foot. And by focusing on gratitude, we successfully made it through a challenging time. Our team became stronger as we familiarized ourselves with new tasks and streamlined various processes. Now tasks are well defined and we have a backup for each function. The tough growing pains were worth it; we are in a better place than ever before and more equipped to handle any challenges.

"Life's challenges
are not supposed
to paralyze you,
they're supposed
to help you
**discover
who you are.**"

~Bernice Johnson Reagon

People Challenges

It is fascinating how the concepts I wrote about in my book, *Culture Infusion*, have expanded since 2017 with practice. In that book, I gave the example of Thich Nhat Hanh's Watering the Flowers exercise (from his books *A Pebble for Your Pocket*[20] and *The Art of Communicating*[21]), in which one is invited to start any difficult conversation with gratitude.

Watering the Flowers suggests three questions: What are you grateful for? What do you regret? How were your feelings hurt?

When I wrote *Culture Infusion*, I had only used Hanh's strategy a few times at work. Now it is second nature. I have also since modified the exercise to meet our needs and tailored it to a business setting.

When we have two or more people dealing with a conflict at Actualize, this is how I apply the exercise. First, I talk to each person separately to get their side of the story. Second, I ask them if they would be willing to walk through an exercise with each person involved on the phone or in person, depending on geographic locations. I explain that I will guide them through four questions:

1. What are you grateful for about the person and this experience?

2. What have you contributed to the situation, and what would you have changed about your approach?

3. How did the situation make you feel?

4. How would you like to move forward in a positive light, and what will you commit to going forward?

Once the involved parties agree to try this method, I give them time to think through the questions and answer them with only me. As they vent their frustration to me, it allows and validates their feelings, clears their mind, and opens room for empathy. They now have capacity to see the other person's side. Then, once all parties and I are on the conference call or in the meeting, we go through the same questions, starting with gratitude to help create a clean slate and lighten the mood so that a real, growth-inducing conversation can take place.

Gratitude Infusion

At our firm, this exercise led us through a profound experience with a supervisor and direct report. Anger was expressed and tears shed prior to our call. After working through this exercise, the results were astounding. Here is how the conversation went.

1. **Gratitude:** The supervisor shared, "I am very impressed with your will to succeed in your role and your hard-working ethics." The direct report shared, "I recognize you have a lot on your plate, and I see how hard you are working to keep the team together, sell work, and manage our office."

2. **Contribution:** The supervisor reflected, "In a few cases, I got angry and I should have been more patient with you, because you are new to consulting." The direct report reflected, "I am very emotional, and I should have not taken your feedback so personally."

3. **Feel:** They both said they felt like they could work together in a positive light now.

4. **Move Forward:** We decided it was best to move the person to another supervisor who had more time to work with someone new to consulting.

As we were ending the call, I could sense that the relationship of the supervisor and direct report had changed as they laughed and talked shop about project work and logistics. They now have a strong working relationship because they handled the conflict head-on. Employing gratitude as a tactic immediately lightens the mood of any tense situation and clears a path for problem solving and understanding.

GRATITUDE-EXPANDING EXPERIENCES

Personal: Go back to a recent challenge you experienced. Reflect on how you dealt with the challenge. How could you have handled it differently? Can you find something to be grateful for from the experience? What lessons will you take with you to be able to handle challenges more effectively in the future?

Workplace: Do you have any current challenges you are facing as a team? If so, how can you incorporate gratitude to move forward in a positive light?

Gratitude Infusion: Reflect on how using gratitude in challenges would benefit your organization. How can you start leading by example in dealing with challenges and training your leaders to do the same?

CHAPTER 8

Award with Gratitude

Do you remember the last time you felt truly appreciated? You might think we don't need to hear words of appreciation, but psychologist and physician William James says, "The deepest craving of human nature is the need to be appreciated." Giving and receiving feelings of gratitude and appreciation can elevate dopamine levels, increasing motivation, focus, and mood.

Just because gratitude is extremely important, however, doesn't mean that we always receive it. I find that corporate environments are especially lacking in appreciation for their employees. The first time I truly felt that a company authentically cared and recognized team efforts was when I briefly worked at a startup technology company that is still thriving to this day. I left because they asked me to relocate to another office; otherwise I would have stayed—it felt like home to me, and I knew my work was valued.

Working for that startup greatly affected the way I show up in the world, as all life experiences do. I use that as well as my past experience working for other firms as guideposts for my leadership style, emulating what those companies did well. Here are three examples of what worked in the technology company:

1. **On-boarding:** They took the time to ensure we knew the culture, the mission, and the value of what they were offering. I remember it was a new technology and I had to give a presentation to pitch the company. To be able to make a pitch, I had to learn from the start about how the company wanted us to portray their message in a cohesive way.

2. **Shout-outs:** We were encouraged to email companywide shout-outs to our peers when they did a good job. On a busy day, we received *at least* one or two emails of gratitude toward peers. It gave a sense of home, and even the smallest tasks were recognized.

3. **Support:** Given the nature of the business, the company had to provide weekend support for our clients. When the service was not working for one of my clients, I worked all weekend with the technical team to resolve the issue. My manager stepped in to help on Sunday because he said I needed a break. His offer to help was not expected, and it made me feel as though we were more than just a team—we were a family.

What I have witnessed and personally felt is that we are more inclined to be our best, go out of the way for others, and be a team player when we feel safe and supported. It goes back to Maslow's hierarchy of needs.

MASLOW'S HIERARCHY OF NEEDS

- **Self-Actualization:** Wishing to realize one's full potential

- **Esteem:** Valuing oneself

- **Love and Belonging:** Receiving love and acceptance from others

- **Safety Needs:** Having a sense of security

- **Physiological Needs:** Having ample food, water, shelter

With our jobs, we earn money to take care of our basic needs, fulfilling the bottom level of the pyramid. But as we climb higher, we crave a sense of belonging. Many times, it is easier to feel that on a personal level, but that doesn't always happen at work. At Actualize, we strive to create a home for our employees so that they feel they belong. You can feel respected when you are recognized for being your best; this is how we fulfill employees' need for self-actualization. That is not a coincidence. Our Founding Partner— my brother, Chad Wekelo—built the company on the foundation that we will be our best for our clients. Our tagline is, "Our expertise and commitment—driving your success."

If you want to help your team self-actualize, remember that when a team member puts extra effort into a project and it goes unnoticed, it can leave them feeling flat. A simple thank you can go a long way. And putting extra effort into a creative show of gratitude can be even more meaningful. Below are some creative ways to show your appreciation for your team members to give them a sense of belonging and recognition, so they will desire to be their best.

Share Gratitude

Because gratitude supports a sense of community, at Actualize, we infuse a culture of gratitude and appreciation through a variety of methods that we will discuss below. The first step is to determine the communication plan to support the actions. Look at your firm's vehicles for communication, and determine the best course of action.

At Actualize, we share internally and publicly via social media. Internally, we start meetings with gratitude, appreciation, and wins. We also send out emails to the team with links to a featured article, podcast, or awards our team or firm has won. We even have a monthly newsletter in which the first section is titled "People." We include items such as:

- Birthdays
- Weddings
- New babies and adoptions
- Pictures from social events

- Updates on team challenges (discussed more in Chapters 5 and 9)

- Awards

- Promotions

Our external sharing on social media is a copy of what we are sharing internally—we use the same images and content. We use LinkedIn as our first priority for sharing. We also have a presence on Facebook, Instagram, and Twitter. Social media is a great tool to proudly appreciate the work of your team.

Now that we have discussed how to share, let's explore some ways to infuse awarding your team in gratitude.

Create Categories of Gratitude

Think about your team's attributes and create categories that let you showcase their skills along with your gratitude. You can keep the same categories every year or change it up. We like to keep it fresh. One year, we put our team members in various consulting categories and thanked them for their contributions to our firm:

- **Expert:** for those with tenure over 10 years

- **Pro:** for tenure of less than 10 years

- **International:** for our consultants traveling abroad

- **Inventive:** for team members who have helped develop a product

Give Star and Key Player Awards

Allow team members to recognize their co-workers for exceptional performance; invite them to nominate anyone within the firm for any act or initiative that they feel should be recognized and celebrated. Awards can be for an ingenious solution to a problem or exceptional teamwork. You can give a monetary bonus or recognition to the star player. Announce the good news to your firm via newsletters, email blasts, and company meetings. Take the accolades a step further and post publicly on social media.

- The **Star Player** program allows Actualize team members to recognize their co-workers for exceptional performance.

- The **Key Player** program is a way to recognize those who are fundamental in assisting with an internal initiative or mentoring at Actualize.

At Actualize, employees may submit a nomination via email describing what the nominee did and why that qualifies them as a Star Player or Key Player.

Example Star Player Nomination: I wanted to recommend Jack for a Star Player award. We have been working together on our client for the last year or so, and the client has proven quite challenging in a number of ways, ranging from evolving requirements to less-than-ideal knowledge transfer across regional teams. Jack's tenacity and creative approach to problem solving has allowed us to bring the project nearly to a close, building a strong relationship between our team and theirs in the meantime. We would not be in that position without his contributions, often putting in extra time to resolve client requests.

Example Key Player Nomination: Rad was recruited to act as a co-ordinator and troubleshooter-in-chief for one of our projects, and, despite having limited subject matter experience, Rad caught up and quickly became indispensable. He was faced not just with a steep technical learning curve but also with poorly coordinated client stakeholders and constantly shifting priorities. Rad might have been the single biggest factor in rescuing several workstreams and earning the client's trust in our team. I'd like to nominate him for the Key Player award.

Here are sample social media graphics for the Star Player and Key Player Awards.

BEST PRACTICE GUIDE

STAR PLAYERS

Jason Blumstein, Cecilia Chan, John
Kruger, Eric Meis, Priscila Nagalli,
Brian Stitt, Hubert Sy, Maddie
Yaskowski, Rena Zhou

KEY PLAYERS

Craig Chapman, Claudio Delgado, Yen
Hew, Danny Kaplan, Alysia Kennedy,
Kyle Olovson, Will Robertson, Aaron
Russell, Tyler Sciortino, Sandra Shen,
Jack Su, Mike Wisniowski, Doug York

Performance Bonus

Actions and words are profound when it comes to gratitude. And to help meet our employees' basic needs, monetary awards can also show our gratitude. At Actualize, we like to reward for performance to show that no hard work goes unnoticed. It is our way of giving back to our team. We pay performance bonuses twice a year—on July 15 and December 31. The bonus process in other firms where I worked was ever-changing and never certain, but we have made sure that ours is transparent and steady. Our team knows they will be rewarded for going above and beyond.

Actualize Awards

Interestingly enough, Actualize Consulting has received awards as a company as well. It started with receiving the Healthiest Company Award, which was an application process that did not include surveying our employees. After winning that award, we searched for more meaningful accomplishments, ones that actually put our culture to the test with anonymous surveys. To date, we have received three corporate culture awards: Top Company Culture by *Entrepreneur* magazine, Top Workplace by the *Washington Post,* and a Great Place to Work-Certification by Great Place to Work.

The Great Place to Work certification that we received in 2020 was even more special because they created a word cloud of key themes in our employees' survey answers. In the picture below, you can see the words "people," "wellness," and "culture" as major motifs. In 2010, we had set the intention to focus on our people. Ten years later, we are still reaping the rewards of an employee-focused business.

A recent client asked me after an initial team-building session, "How do you keep the momentum going?"

"With hard work and dedication," I said.

However, it wasn't until I saw the visual above that I realized the full power and meaning of why I use the word "infusion" for culture and gratitude. Gratitude and culture cannot be sprinkled on top; it must be layered throughout your organization. When you take the time to infuse appreciation and healthy culture into your organization, I promise you that gratitude will be rewarded and matched.

Actualize recently received the following kudos from one of our Senior Consultants, Aaron Russell: "Actualize is a great place to work because leadership (and everyone else) has put the time, energy, and effort into making this a great place to work. I appreciate the effort that everyone has put into this company, and that effort has made following the leaders very easy. Great work!!"

GRATITUDE-EXPANDING EXPERIENCES

Personal: When was a time you fully felt heartfelt gratitude expressed to you? How did it feel?

Workplace: Based on their work in the last month, who on your team would you give a Star Player award to? Even if you cannot formally give the award, how can you express your gratitude to them for going above and beyond? Hint: Give them a call, take them out to lunch, or send an email or hand-written card and let them know why you believe they are a Star Player.

Gratitude Infusion: What current awards do you have in your firm? How can you incorporate gratitude into your reward system?

CHAPTER 9

Give Back

Giving back will always have a special place in my heart. My first heartwarming memories come from giving back and helping others. One of the ways I shift my perspective when I am feeling down is by experiencing the full force of humility when I give back. It works like a charm to see faces light up and moods lift when I help others, and it is one of the reasons I specifically enjoy hands-on giving. To me, hands-on giving means being physically present for my donation and donating my time in addition to any other monetary or material contributions. For example, I enjoy making lunches for the homeless shelter I support. My kids and I, along with team members from Actualize Consulting, have been making these lunches since 2015. We gather in my home to prepare the lunches, and then we deliver them to the shelter. I love seeing the impact we can have on other people.

My childhood friend, who suffered with cancer for ten years until she passed away before turning seventeen, truly shaped how fortunate I feel each and every day. When you see another human struggling, whether for their life or to meet their daily sustenance needs, you quickly recognize that you are not the only one with struggles. We all have hard times, struggles, and pain, and it is working through our own pain that makes us even stronger. That friend, Jennifer, left an imprint on my heart. I learned to keep moving forward no matter what is in front of me. And by practicing gratitude, it is easier to see the big picture in every struggle I face.

"Jennifer left an imprint on my heart. **I learned to keep moving forward** no matter what is in front of me."

Over the years I have supported Cornerstones in Virginia and the Doe Fund in New York, and seeing the experiences of the homeless and their fight to get back on their feet firsthand is incredibly humbling. My senses are enhanced each time I walk into one of the shelters; I breathe the stale air and feel the heaviness of defeat and sadness mixed with the hope that tomorrow will be a better day.

One memory of hope that stands out to me is from my visit to a shelter with rooms designated specifically for families who need food and housing. The shelter does the best they can to give presents and support families over the holidays. One way they work at that is to schedule volunteers to play with the children while their parents have a night out. I signed up to play and laugh with the kids, trying to lift their spirits as we were entering the holiday season.

I quickly recognized there were four siblings present for the family I was helping. The oldest girl was quiet and kept to herself in another corner of the room. I could see that she was struggling to put on a happy face. Her loneliness and longing for "normal" teenage years were evident. After I lost a game of Connect Four to one of her siblings and knew I had little time left to spend with the girl, I slowly walked over to her. I began a conversation by sharing some things about myself and my life. I told her that I have two children and that I love to explore new places. She remained silent, steel walls up, and did not even acknowledge my presence. Bringing out my Zendoway Feelings Cube[22]—a soft, squeezable cube made out of stress ball foam with prompts on each side—I said to her, "I love to create, and I made this cube. I want you to have it."

She turned her head slightly to make eye contact, and as I peered into her eyes, I saw a way to connect. She said, "Really, you made this? Why? How? What do you even do with it?"

"Do you want to give it a try?" I asked.

She rolled the cube and read the prompts. Then she began to open up and share her feelings with me. (The prompts are in italics and her answers in bold.)

- *I wonder:* **When will we have a home?**

- *I love:* **My family.**

- *I am grateful:* **For this shelter that has rooms for our family so we can have some space. Other shelters do not have rooms for families.**

- *I feel:* **Confused. Why does our family have to struggle so much?**

- *I am proud:* **Of my mom for leaving our abusive father. I would rather be homeless than unsafe.**

- *I see:* **My brother and sisters having fun, and that you actually care about us.**

By giving this teenage girl the space to be vulnerable, she felt safe enough to express herself to a caring adult. This encounter and countless others are why I am passionate about hands-on giving. Yes, I could give a check and walk away. That would certainly be helpful, and monetary donations are powerful gifts. However, I would not gain the richness of giving back to others. Emmons states in his *Little Book of Gratitude*, "Gratitude makes those who receive grace long to give it back. In giving back the good, gratitude becomes thanksgiving and the cycle between receiving and giving is completed."[23] The truth of this quote resonates with every cell in my body. When we give, we receive much more in return.

In *Culture Infusion*,[24] I talk about the need to be myself in all aspects of my life. Because of my personal passion for giving back, I incorporated that as part of our culture at Actualize Consulting. Now we are not only giving back but also getting to know each other better while having a positive impact on the world. Given the relatively small size of our organization, with fewer than 100 employees, we faced a lot of naysayers in the beginning. People would tell us that because we are such a small firm it would be impossible for us to make a "big" impact. At that point, I decided that no matter how "big" our impact, we could at least make a lasting one on our surrounding communities with a creative hands-on giving approach.

The bonds I have formed with our teams over the years while giving back are memories I cherish. Years ago, for example, we hosted a wellness event for underprivileged schoolchildren, where we read and played with the children. We did this as a team and had a blast joining together to give back. I remember seeing one of our team members in a totally different light after I witnessed him reading to the children. At work, we are always in go-mode, and we often do not fully see each other. In the vulnerability of sharing with others, our true, authentic bright light shines.

That day transformed my view of not just him but our entire team. We bonded. We shared. We gave back. It was humbling for all of us. We knew those kids were going home to environments where they didn't have the same kind of basic-need security that we were so fortunate to have.

Giving Back at Work

At Actualize Consulting, giving back is one of the foundational principles of our corporate culture, starting with ourselves and our employees, then spreading out to our clients. It doesn't stop there, though. We believe in also sharing our success by giving back in ways that are truly helpful to our local community. We have infused a culture of hands-on giving with opportunities for our team to give back. Below are some examples of our programs to inspire you and your teams.

At the Client Level

Our clients sustain us, motivate us, push us to succeed, and provide so many reasons for us to enjoy our work. For all they give to us, we definitely want to give back to them and make sure they know we don't take them for granted. Our communications as a firm focus not only on our people but also our clients. We like to go out of our way to ensure client satisfaction. Instead of waiting for the holidays to show appreciation, we like to do so year-round. Our internal team sends company swag and personalized thank you notes when clients are not expecting them. We also send employees simple reminders of ways to build relationships with clients, such as sharing relevant industry articles and going above and beyond on a simple task—we want our clients to know we handle each task efficiently and accurately no matter the level of importance.

We also strive to host client appreciation events to allow people from all the firms we work with to network and have fun. We have gone with clients to sporting and entertainment events such as basketball and Cirque du Soleil, hosted happy hours, and invited industry speakers to knowledge share. Because of this, we have high retention rates with our clients. We infuse client satisfaction into our culture, which shows up in excellent client satisfaction ratings.

At a Team Level

On a team level, there are many ways to encourage giving back. Here are a few examples based on what we have done at Actualize.

Inspired by Valentine's Day, I created the Intentional Acts of Kindness Challenge.[25] Whenever someone goes out of their way to help me, it brightens my mood for the rest of the day, so I decided to multiply the good cheer. To get in the spirit of sharing and spreading love, I recruited the help of the firm and added a dash of competition for team bonding by splitting participants into teams of five. For every act of kindness completed, employees would earn one point. The goal was for each person to contribute at least one point per week to their team for the challenge. The prizes for the teams with the most points at the end of the month included a choice of extra wellness or training dollars. We even partnered with the Doe Fund to create a wish list of necessary items to donate and matched every employee donation.

It was a fun way to give back. Our entire team bonded over acts of kindness, and it was so empowering to see the various ways our people were giving back to their communities:

- Leaving snacks out for the mailman or package carrier
- Sharing a meal with a neighbor
- Volunteering at a shelter
- Donating old clothes

- Donating blood

- Making treats as a thank you

- Volunteering at a nearby school

Bonding over Isolation

When the COVID-19 pandemic officially hit the United States in 2020, Actualize was in the midst of its March Madness–themed wellness challenge. Each team, comprised of five employees, was competing remotely to earn points for different healthy actions, like eating five servings of fruits and vegetables, trying a new exercise, exercising for 30 minutes a day, stretching, and more. To liven up the competition, Jason Blumstein, Senior Manager, proposed a challenge to his team: he would give $0.50 to Meals on Wheels for each pushup done by a team member. In total, his team of five people ended up doing 444 pushups, so Jason donated $222!

Inspired by Jason, I did a similar challenge with my team. For every new activity they tried, I would donate $10 and if they sent in a video, I'd donate $20 to Meals on Wheels. It was so encouraging to see how our teams could pull together to give back to a worthy cause while practicing physical distancing. It is important to be grateful for all we have, even when surrounded by tragedy. We are fortunate to still have our jobs, to have family, to have friends—the list goes on. Sometimes giving back doesn't have to be planned; you can make it a fun spur-of the-moment activity.

Corporate Social Responsibility

As Daniel Goleman, author of books such as *Focus* and *Emotional Intelligence*, said, "One aspect of wisdom is having a very wide horizon which doesn't center on ourselves." I'd like to add to this: it doesn't even center on our own group or organization. Actualize puts that theory into action by encouraging participation in activities that support social causes and help us extend our horizon of awareness. Throughout the year, we give back to the community in creative and hands-on ways. For each organization we support, we truly act as their partner. I personally meet with each organization annually to determine the best way we can support them in the coming year. Below are some examples of our hands-on giving.

The Doe Fund

The Doe Fund is a non-profit organization that helps men who have faced homelessness, addiction, and incarceration rebuild their lives by providing housing, paid work, career counseling, and education opportunities.

Tasks we have helped with include:

- Collecting vegetables for a senior center in Harlem
- Conducting mock interviews for those ready to reenter the workforce
- Making scarves to help keep workers warm in the winter months as they clean New York streets and perform other outside paid tasks sponsored by the program (This project ended up being one of our most successful to date; collectively, Actualize has hand-sewed and embroidered 245 scarves to donate!)
- Creating holiday care packages with essential items such as water bottles, shaving kits, and toiletries
- Contributing to an Amazon Wish List of business clothes (shirts, pants, belts, shoes, reading glasses) for interviews

Because of our hands-on approach, we were awarded the distinction of an Honorary Ready, Willing & Able Graduate, similar to how universities give honorary diplomas to those who have made contributions to society. What an honor for us.

To learn more about the Doe Fund, visit https://www.doe.org/.

Cornerstones

Cornerstones is a non-profit organization that helps those in need of food, shelter, and affordable housing. At Actualize, we help donate monthly lunches to serve 60 people, holiday gifts for kids, and bedding and clothes for families.

To learn more about Cornerstones, visit https://www.cornerstonesva.org/.

Alex's Lemonade Stand

We use Alex's Lemonade Stand's Million Mile as part of our annual September Wellness Challenge.[26] This charity strives to raise money to fund childhood cancer research. The goal of Million Mile is for everyone on the platform to collectively walk, bike, run, or swim 1,000,000 miles as they pledge and fundraise per mile. We have found that tying a give-back initiative to our wellness challenge provides extra motivation and keeps us focused on a collective cause. It also attaches a sense of responsibility. Actualize usually offers a donation match to encourage employees to participate.

To learn more about Alex's Lemonade Stand, visit https://www.alexslemonade.org/.

The Value of Hands-On Giving

Hands-on giving is clearly a hit among employees and has helped us at Actualize learn a number of ways it is valuable.

It's a way to relax and spend time with loved ones.

In such a go-go-go society, it can be hard to find time to unwind and catch up with those who are important to you. Hands-on giving is a catalyst for finding that time. It's not something you can do and just forget about; it takes effort and love.

You can set aside the time to relax by yourself, or invite some of your friends to help. One of Actualize's team members who sewed scarves with a friend discovered how precious such time could be: "I always get more than I give when I volunteer," she said. "This time, I got to spend time with a dear friend who is now thousands of miles away. We will both remember how much fun we had together while sewing scarves."

You feel connected to those you are supporting.

Especially with gifts that are tangible, you can see the difference you are making in others' lives. The scarves, for example, will provide warmth for 245 people—warmth provided by the material itself as well as from the personal touch of those who made and embroidered the scarves. The impact of this kind of personal touch is difficult to put into words. In this case, it was maybe a little like sending 245 handwritten letters versus emails—it takes a little more effort and the message lasts longer.

Employees also recruited their friends and family to help and used giving back as a theme to fuel their fellowship.[27] For one Actualize employee who made scarves with her mother-in-law, she said she felt uplifted with gratitude: "The Doe Fund is a special organization that myself and my family are excited to continue to support," she said. "Hopefully, these gentlemen know how proud we are of them and how grateful we are to be a part of their journey."

It connects members of the community through a common goal.

If you have a hands-on giving-back idea, try reaching out to your neighbors and friends to see if they would like to help. The spirit of giving should be shared, and it can also be a great way to support small businesses. A friend of an employee said, "By working on these scarves, I was not only able to earn to help my home—being disabled, this was huge for my psyche—but I was also able to create, which is something I thrive on. Most importantly, however, I was able give back to some very important gentlemen deserving of a little extra warmth. It was my honor to have made these scarves with my hands, but best of all, with all my heart."

How to Get Started

Desiring to give back is really the first step—once you have a passion for spreading love, you are already halfway there. Maybe you have a cause already in mind that is near and dear to your business, or perhaps you want to reach out to your team for ideas. You may want to begin by examining your existing giving-back and cause-related programs and surveying your teams on what inspires them. With everyone's feedback in mind, you can start tailoring a custom game plan that infuses giving back as a part of your social footprint. Not only will you receive fresh ideas, but you also might be able to align individual interests with company goals.

Be sure to have a team member take the lead for each event to ensure all is well-organized. Additionally, determine the best way to track your results. Alex's Lemonade Stand, for example, provides an online tracking tool. For our Intentional Acts of Kindness Challenge, we used Google Sheets to track our progress since the files are easy to access and share.

- Survey your people to find out what types of organizations or specific organizations they would like to see your firm supporting.

- Connect with organizations to see if there is a way you can best support their needs.

- Align your fundraising or time donations with a team challenge.

- Share the results and announce the winning team on social media and in newsletters.

Keep the Fire Going

The idea of giving back isn't just a "one and done" activity; we need to keep finding ways to fuel the giving-back fire. At Actualize, gratitude is a fuel for that fire, and it's endlessly renewable.

"Cultivate the habit
of **being grateful** for
every good thing that comes
to you, and to **give thanks**
continuously. And because
all things have contributed to
your advancement, you should
include all things in
in your gratitude."

~Ralph Waldo Emerson

Usually, at the end of each challenge, we ask our employees to say what they are grateful for. It may be the end of the challenge, but it keeps them forward thinking and leaves them with gratitude on their mind. For example, here are some responses we collected at the end of our previous challenge.

"I'm grateful that I have
the resolution to be grateful.
Being grateful motivates me and
keeps me focused on what's good
in the world."

"Today I am definitely grateful to have
a career that makes me proud; the kindness of
strangers during the holidays; the many sites
I see daily for donations; health and happiness
surrounding my friends and family..."

"...for working with this great group of
professionals that make up the Actualize family.
**By far the best company I've
ever worked for...** Thanks,
everybody for all your
help and the positive
attitude that you bring
on a daily basis..."

At Actualize, we have found that even a small company can have a huge impact when all levels of leadership and employees truly care about and are united in making a positive difference. I encourage you to infuse gratitude into the operations of your firm. It brings people together, provides inspiration, and makes a positive difference for employees, your company, and your community.

GRATITUDE-EXPANDING EXPERIENCES

Personal: When you think about giving back in your life, what has given you the most joy? Make a list of ways to share your time and talent with others. In the next month, make a plan to give back in a way that feels good to you.

Workplace: What personal interests do you share with your team? How could you and your team give back together? For example, if you share in enjoying movement, perhaps participate in a charity walk or align yourself with a national organization like Alex's Lemonade Stand.

Gratitude Infusion: Examine your company's current giving-back program. What changes could you make to engage your entire firm and enhance your culture with a theme of giving back?

CHAPTER 10

Gratitude in Uncertain Times

At the time this book went to the line editor, the world as we knew it had changed with COVID-19. Virginia and many other US states were under a stay-at-home order; we were no longer allowed to come and go as we please, and soon the only outings allowed were for essential reasons. Together, the United States and the rest of the world faced uncharted waters. I began to feel suffocated and my survival instinct took over, willing me to focus on forward movement. In Chapter 7, Handle Challenges with Gratitude, I mentioned how life will always bring trials. This virus was undoubtedly a trial that no one had planned for, nor were we able to comprehend how it could both stop the world and unite us on a common problem. During the pandemic, I tried my best to use my 3P Method. I found myself spending significant time in the pause. I found that challenging my creative energy by uplifting my family and Actualize team was the best way for me to keep my spirits high. I wanted to share some of the ways we came together as a more cohesive team during this uncertain time.

Grateful for Our People

Each year, Actualize has an annual retreat in which we bring all of our offices together for a long weekend of bonding. Because of COVID-19, we are uncertain if we will be able to hold one in 2020. However, I wanted to make sure we still celebrated our people. We surveyed the team, asking them if there was any gratitude that they had to share about each other. I was sitting with their responses and my own feelings of gratitude for our people, yet I wanted to share in a meaningful and unique way. I decided to create videos for each person and team. With the help of Maddie Yaskowski, one of my internal team members, we used videos I recorded, fun pictures from previous events, and the words of others to bring the gratitude to life as best we could since not be together. We were sure to include everyone on the team. We are so lucky to live in an age where technology is so readily available, allowing us to still connect with others virtually.

One example was the celebration of Tom Sitzler and Victor Olivo for being with Actualize for 10 years. Below are some of the fun pictures included in the video.

Connecting During Isolation

As I witnessed the world coming together, the same was happening with our team at Actualize. In the past, I tried to check in and have connections with all of our people. This type of connection is part of our culture. With COVID-19, I found myself taking even more time to check in. Each day presents different challenges for each person. Many of our team members had family that had the virus, babies born, and family members sick with other ailments. On top of that, one of our key locations in New York was hit hard. I truly was worried about everyone's safety. I changed my sign-off in emails to "stay safe." My mama bear need was even stronger. It was critical for my well-being to be more mindful and empathic to each person I spoke to daily. With more time on my hands with only essential outings being made and most of my kids' activities canceled, I wanted to focus my energy in a positive way. The question I was asking myself was, "How does Actualize keep its team connected throughout this period of isolation?" Below are some of the ways we strengthened our bond and got to know each other better.

Scheduling Mindful Breaks: It's important to denote that "mindful" doesn't have to mean its definition in the traditional sense. While it definitely can mean guided meditation or breathing exercises, it can also just mean a good icebreaker with some hearty laughs. Once a week, we had a firm-wide Zoom call with a different theme. Examples include guided breathing, two truths and one lie, wearing your favorite pair of sunglasses, show and tell, sharing your favorite joke – anything to have a fun team moment and keep connected. We also incorporated virtual happy hours and lunches.

Having an Open-Door Policy: Our leadership team has always had an open-door policy, but it was more important than ever that people knew this was still available, especially with many new struggles. We always encourage employees to come to us with their issues – perhaps they need more flexibility in their schedules, or maybe they just need some ideas for how to tackle a current challenge. As a mom who has 15 years' experience working from home and raising children, I have many ideas for our working parents and can help them problem solve. No matter the issue at hand, and whether it's during a pandemic or not, we want our employees to know that we are willing to brainstorm and work with them to ensure it gets resolved.

Keeping Open Communication: With the state of the economy at the time, people were feeling very uncertain about their employment status. Many companies were laying people off and furloughing, which can be very unsettling for everyone who relies on a paycheck to feed their families. No matter what you have to do to keep your business afloat, it is important to make sure your employees are aware of big picture decisions being made. At the beginning of the pandemic, Actualize was very lucky that we still had new business coming in and that we did not need to think about reducing our team. We sent out a firm-wide letter from leadership to make sure everyone was aware of this – it was a collective deep breath for many of our employees, especially our newer hires who were feeling stressed. But even if it was bad news that needed to be delivered, your team should hear it from leadership versus rumors and assumptions.

To help provide even more updates, we also began upping our monthly newsletters to semi-monthly. In these newsletters, we list our firm "wins" and new clients. It's a great way to boost morale, especially so everyone is able to see that we are still successful amid the faltering economy.

Encouraging Giving Back: During the pandemic, everyone was in this together. It was a time to support small businesses if you could, help others who lacked food security, lend a hand to a neighbor, and more. Even if you are unable to donate monetarily, you can help someone else with your gifts and talents. Giving back can be so inspiring and help you stay grounded in gratitude for what you have.

Allowing Humor: Some people have different ways of coping with trauma. Humor is one of these methods. We now have a Google Group dedicated to jokes and memes where people can post and share funny stories, videos, and photos. It might not seem like a major addition to our firm, but it does allow for some fun and reminds us that there is always light in the darkness.

I learned through this uncertain time that gratitude expands through getting to know each other better. In the world before COVID-19, we were busy and many times not mindful of others. The true gift of the pandemic was extra time to bond and get to know our loved ones, and remind ourselves of what is really important in life.

GRATITUDE-EXPANDING EXPERIENCES

Personal: How has your gratitude expanded in uncertain times?

Workplace: What did your team do to come together during the time of remote working? What changes will you make or have you made to continue getting to know your team?

Gratitude Infusion: What has changed for the better for your company during uncharted waters? How will you use the power of gratitude to ensure your company stays connected as a whole?

CHAPTER 11

Grateful Companies in Action

When I started incorporating gratitude into my personal life and shifting our culture at Actualize to put our people first, it felt as though I was in my own personal Kerry bubble. It was a struggle to keep up the positivity and focus on gratitude without much support. We were still a new company trying to navigate a challenging major culture rehaul.

Along this journey, however, I noticed my Gratitude Bubble expanding and attracting. I have been fortunate to meet and collaborate with others who share in the vision of gratitude and recognize its powerful force. In this chapter, I share experiences and wisdom from other people who have found success implementing gratitude into their work culture and life. Each profile includes a description of how they have impacted me personally and their answers to a series of questions. If you wish to connect further with any of these gratitude practitioners, I've also provided their contact information.

I am grateful to each one of these extraordinary individuals. And remember—the more you share your passion and vision with others, the more people you can reach. Practice gratitude by reaching out to those you admire and whose vision you share; be generous in supporting them and others in your network, just as I've done here.

Name: Lisa Ryan

Company: Grategy

Personal Impact: I have subscribed to Lisa's "Gratitude Thought of the Week" newsletter since 2012, early in my quest for creating and maintaining thriving organizational cultures. Lisa has diligently shared and inspired me for years. I did not reach out to her until I wanted to include her in this book. In hindsight, I should have let her know much sooner how grateful I was for this weekly dose of gratitude in my inbox.

What does gratitude mean to you?

Gratitude is being able to look for and find the good in every situation, no matter what is going on. It's a focus on the things that you have, instead of what's missing in your life. It's an opportunity to pause and reflect on the blessings you have in your life and to acknowledge the people, places, and things that are making a positive difference to you every day.

Why did you start the movement? Why did you include gratitude as a key component?

I started a gratitude practice with some friends after a four-day workshop. I went into it with no expectations—we were simply sharing three things with each other every day for which we were grateful. I noticed so many differences in my life as a result of my practice that I knew that this was a message I needed to share with the world. Gratitude is not just a feel-good emotion. It's scientifically proven to help us be healthier, happier, more prosperous, and more positive in everything we do. It heals relationships and makes the good ones even better. Simply put, gratitude works!

What have you gained by shifting your focus to gratitude?

My marriage is stronger than ever, I have great relationships with my family members, my business is thriving, and when something "bad" happens, I automatically look for the good—current or future—that will come out of the situation.

What difference has this made on your life?

It's made a huge difference. Ten years of keeping a gratitude journal has changed the wiring in my brain, and now I focus on the good.

What difference has this made on the lives of others?

The simple strategies that I share with my audience, participants, and clients give them accessible ideas that they can easily implement. I have the privilege of hearing their stories every week when my "Gratitude Thought of the Week" comes out every Thursday—as it's been doing since 2011.

How would you suggest an individual get started with adding gratitude into their life?

Get a notebook or journal, and every morning, before your feet hit the floor, reach over, take your journal and write down 3–5 things for which you are grateful. You can actually be grateful in advance of the day and set a positive expectation for things to come. In the evening, you can also look back on the day and write down 3–5 good things that happened to you.

How would you suggest a company incorporate gratitude into their culture?

Start meetings on a positive note. Encourage people to share 30 seconds of good news before getting down to business. Encourage peer-to-peer recognition to acknowledge each other's efforts. Provide thank you notes or some kind of "kudos" cards so people can catch each other in the act of doing things well. Focus on what is going well in the organization, and try to do more of that—instead of always focusing on what's broken and needs to be "fixed."

What other easy infusions, in addition and similar to gratitude, would you suggest for improving Culture?

It's not necessarily easy, but leadership buy-in is critical. If managers believe that gratitude/employee engagement initiatives are a "human resource matter" and they are not invested in the process themselves, they are setting themselves and their organization up for failure. Also, the realization that culture takes a long time to build—and it's not going to change overnight. You must be patient with the process and learn your lessons along the way. Getting feedback on your initiatives and acting on the recommendations is also important.

Contact:

lisa@grategy.com

www.LisaRyanSpeaks.com

Name: Darin Hollingsworth

Company: Odonata Coaching & Consulting

Personal Impact: I love Darin's podcast, *Working Gratitude*, and his work. Darin's positive outlook inspires me each time I listen to his podcast or read his writings.

What does gratitude mean to you?

This is a BIG question for me. Gratitude has been part of my life for my memorable life. My parents instilled a core value of gratitude in my brothers and me, exhibited predominately by being required to write thank you notes as soon as we could write. Fast forward to my early career...I realized how unique and rare the handwritten note is, be it for job interviews or with clients/donors. I got GREAT feedback from the simple act of writing a note of thanks—for time, investment, or just inspiring my work.

In a lifelong struggle to maintain mental health and at times heal mental illness—severe depression, anxiety, and more recently, PTSD—I have found that when I can get back to my gratitude practice, no matter how "small" the thing I am grateful for is, I begin the shift back toward focus on health.

Gratitude has truly changed my life and work...many times.

Why did you start the movement? Why did you include gratitude as a key component?

I started my podcast, _Working Gratitude—Real People. Real Gratitude at Work._, back in 2012. So, was it a movement? Back then you still had to download podcasts to a proprietary device...and truly I don't know how many people listened. Analytics were not as readily available to the amateur content creator back then. But I believed passionately in the focus on bringing gratitude to the workplace. The real science-based evidence for gratitude was still emerging.

In 2012, I attended a Pathways to Gratefulness summit created and hosted by A Network for Grateful Living. To say that I was inspired and found my place and a calling is an understatement. I had been in a gratitude practice of my own for some time. Numerous books, books on CD, blogs, etc. from spiritual teachers and thought leaders had inspired me. What struck me most was a panel at the summit that included BUSINESS leaders who were bringing gratitude (and mindfulness) into the board room and to their employees.

I studied, read, and tried to take in every bit of information I could. It seemed, at that time, that there was still a gap in the content around gratitude in the workplace. One of the most definitive works then and now _was 5 Languages of Appreciation in the Workplace_ authored by Dr. Paul White and co-authored with Dr. Gary Chapman, the author of the very popular _5 Love Languages._

Not feeling qualified or inspired to write a book at that time, I thought, "Let's start some conversations around gratitude in the workplace." And thus, *Working Gratitude* was born.

As for why I focused on gratitude, I had proven in my life and in my research that gratitude is a shifting and transformative value and emotion.

What have you gained by shifting your focus to gratitude?

The people and relationships that gratitude conversations have drawn to my life are undoubtedly my greatest gain. Personally, and professionally. I have gained confidence to follow and share this passion.

What difference has this made on your life?

As I mentioned before, gratitude is a transformer and shifter in my life. After a severe and disabling mental health crisis in 2018, it was when I could get back to gratitude, slowly and full of grace, that I turned a corner toward healing.

What difference has this made on the lives of others?

Clients, family, and friends have shared numerous personal stories and professional successes that they attribute to practicing gratitude. I founded and co-moderate a Facebook group called Art of Gratitude. I work to push content that is heart-filled and also science-based. We encourage others to share anything they believe is a creative expression of gratitude—their own or someone else's.

Gratitude Infusion

How would you suggest an individual get started with adding gratitude into their life?

Be intentional. Start at your own pace. Be sincere. Start. Practice. Start over when necessary.

How would you suggest a company incorporate gratitude into their culture?

Here are some very cool resources to check out:

<u>Appreciation at Work</u> *by Dr. Paul White*: As a certified trainer and student of the work of Dr. Paul White, I believe this is one of the most successful ways to bring this work to the workplace.

<u>Gratitude at Work</u> *by Steve Foran*: Steve is a trusted friend, collaborator, and former guest on my podcast. He lives this work and has shared it throughout Canada and beyond.

<u>Greater Good Science Center</u>: Some of the leading research on gratitude and gratitude in the workplace has come from UC Berkeley.

Contact:

<u>https://odonatacoaching.com/working-gratitude</u>

<u>https://www.linkedin.com/company/working-gratitude/</u>

<u>https://odonatacoaching.com/</u>

Name: Steve Foran

Company: Gratitude at Work

Personal Impact: When I was researching other books on gratitude in the workplace, I came across Steve's book *Surviving to Thriving: The 10 Laws of Grateful Leadership*. I was astounded when Steve immediately responded to my inquiry to collaborate. Since then I have been following Steve's work and inspired by his daily gratitude messages. Steve also has introduced me to more in the gratitude community, and I am forever grateful.

What does gratitude mean to you?

Gratitude is the foundational leadership skill for living a thriving life and leading thriving teams. The easiest way to experience gratitude is to see your entire life as a gift. The surest way to see your life as a gift is to develop the daily habit of recording a list of what you're grateful for. Here's the progression:

> *Making a gratitude list daily >> Seeing life as a gift >> Feeling of gratitude >> Thriving happiness*

Why did you start the movement? Why did you include gratitude as a key component?

The dream of One Billion Happier People surfaced when I heard Peter Diamandis answer the question, "How do you determine in what you will invest your time, money, and energy?" His answer was, "I first ask myself if the idea has the potential to impact one billion people." It caused me to ask myself, "Does gratitude have the potential to impact one billion people?" I knew the answer right away and so the dream was born. While I still don't have it fully figured out, I'm closer to knowing today than I was 18 months ago. What I did know then was that it would take more than me, and I believe it will take a movement to make it happen.

What do you offer?

- I make people happy. I teach individuals and organizations why it's important to be grateful, how to be grateful, and most importantly I facilitate experiences where people prove it (the power of gratitude) to themselves. I provide ongoing support to help people maintain a grateful mindset.

- I speak at conferences and corporate events to audiences who want to be happier and for organizations that want more positive, more productive, more innovative, more engaged culture. I facilitate a year-long process to help leadership teams that want to engrain gratitude in their culture.

- I offer online courses that teach the foundational four habits for a grateful mindset and provide a forum for people to connect with other grateful-minded people where they can record, read, and share their gratitudes. I record and share three of my gratitudes every day, and each week we feature a Guest Contributor who shares their gratitudes as well.

What have you gained by shifting your focus to gratitude?

I have strengthened my resilience, and I have gained a growing network of friends and colleagues from around the world who I'm able to learn from and support. I spend less time focused on the negative aspects of life and truly believe it is the source of what feels like unbridled energy.

What difference has this made on the lives of others?

For those who attend our programs, in 90 minutes or less, we see an immediate 15–20 percent improvement on average in how people feel about their life, their colleagues, and their workplace. I'm always getting feedback from people—either by email, voicemail, in person, or on social media—about the impact that gratitude has had on their life. Sometimes it comes years after we first met or crossed paths.

How would you suggest an individual get started with adding gratitude into their life?

Start by recording three things you're grateful for. Don't just think of your gratitude in your head—write it down or record it electronically. The extra step of physically recording it has a greater impact on your mindset. Secondly, start consuming other people's gratitude. A couple ways to do this include: 1) get an accountability partner and share your gratitude with each other daily, and 2) subscribe to a gratitude blog or The Daily Gratitudes (which we offer) so that you can get inspiration, fuel, and perspective. You'll find consuming others' gratitude very helpful on the challenging days in your life when finding gratitude can be difficult.

How would you suggest a company incorporate gratitude into their culture?

A grateful culture begins with individuals who build grateful frames of minds. I recommend that the leadership team begin by establishing their own gratitude practices and then expand it throughout the organization. Bring people together for an inspirational training experience to introduce gratitude into your culture by inviting people to explore how being more intentional with gratitude could help them live a happier, more meaningful life, personally and professionally. Individuals will naturally begin incorporating gratitude practices into the daily operations of the company—like by starting meetings with a roundtable of gratitudes, for example.

Contact:

www.gratitudeatwork.ca

Name: Kevin Monroe

Company: X Factor Consulting and *Higher Purpose Podcast*

Personal Impact: I was a guest on Kevin's *Higher Purpose Podcast*. We hit it off, and I did a Kindness Challenge with his team. This challenge inspired me to live more intentionally. I gain inspiration from Kevin daily.

What does gratitude mean to you?

There was a time in my life, not that long ago, when I thought that gratitude and thankfulness were synonyms. Honestly, I had never given it much thought, but years before, I had a mentor who challenged me to adopt a gratitude habit and "give thanks each day for three things before your feet hit the floor when you're getting out of bed in the morning."

I did that for years.

Well, if I'm honest, I had a very short list of seven or eight things that I rotated in and out of the habit.

Then, back in 2018, I was hosting a 13-week series of challenges that we called The ExtraOrdinary Life Experiment. The goal was to create 13 weekly themes and associated challenges aimed at helping people discover and appreciate the "extra" in what so many consider an otherwise ordinary life.

Naturally, one of the challenges we included we dubbed the Gratitude Challenge because...well, because it sounded better than the Thanksgiving Challenge. That sounded like a turkey-eating contest or something.

Each week for 13 weeks, we created a video about the topic along with some supporting resources that helped people understand the challenge and how to apply it.

When it came time to create the materials for the week devoted to gratitude, that's when **it** happened.

That's when I began pondering the differences between gratitude and thankfulness. Until that time, they existed as synonyms with gratitude obviously being the way to describe an attitude, well, because they rhymed. As a parent, I encouraged my children to have an attitude of gratitude. But if I was hard-pressed to define gratitude, I would default to saying, find something to be thankful for, which is another way of saying what I heard as "count your blessings and quit complaining."

As I pondered the distinctions between the two, it dawned on me that thanksgiving is the act of saying thank you or the expression of thanks. For the first time in my life, I saw gratitude as a mindset, perhaps more accurately, a heart-set.

A lifestyle.

One that includes an awareness that everything in life is a gift. Including the gift of another day. And yes, gratitude includes the giving of thanks and so much more.

That really started me on a journey of gratitude that has become quite phenomenal.

Why did you start the movement? Why did you include gratitude as a key component?

Back in 2017, I had stumbled on two diagrams. I couldn't get them out of my mind. It was two loops that contrasted *scarcity* and *abundance*.

The Scarcity Loop starts with Fear. Fear leads to Anxiety. Anxiety leads to Poor Choices, which lead to Negative Outcomes.

I knew that loop well. I spent a lot of time there, as did the leaders and organizations with which I consulted.

Contrast that with the Abundance Loop that starts with Gratitude. Gratitude produces Peace of Mind. Peace of Mind allows Wise Choices, which lead to Positive Outcomes.

I began incorporating this in my work. And I began starting every conversation or session by asking, "What is something you are grateful for in this moment?"

Not the short list of five, seven, or nine things that you swap out so you sound humble, pious, or grateful. But seriously...pause and ponder, stop, look around. IN THIS MOMENT, what are you grateful for?

Wow! The list began to expand. I started keeping a journal and writing at least three things a day that I am grateful for. Sidenote:

Gratitude Infusion

Earlier today (the day of writing the very words you are reading right now), I made entry number 2,405 in my journal of daily gratitude. Included in today's entries was *laughter*. We had dinner with a group of friends last night and sat outside to eat and enjoy the beautiful weather, which included blue skies and sunshine—two things we've not seen much of lately. There were a couple of moments where we roared with laughter...and it felt good.

Then came an opportunity for a speaking engagement at the national Meals on Wheels conference. I wanted to incorporate gratitude into my presentations and use the loops graphic. There was a line in the contract that I took seriously (like I do all lines in all contracts): If you are using any copyrighted material, you need to attribute the source and have permission to use it.

Well, now I had to find the source.

Several weeks later, I did. It was a book of limited publication by Juliana Park called *The Abundance Loop*. The book was a passion project and not her primary business. I contacted Juliana and shared with her my affinity for her work and secured a copy of her book.

Then I persuaded her to join me as a guest on the Higher Purpose Podcast.

That is when my embrace and understanding of gratitude went to a whole new level.

You see, I discovered that gratitude is the gateway to abundance. In every arena of business, leadership, and life.

As I mentioned, I now begin every consultation by grounding them in the fertile soil of gratitude. And not just that. Every conversation on the podcast. Every coaching call. Every group call I host. We start by somehow grounding in gratitude.

Then, in spring of 2019, I met Steve Foran, who had also written a book on gratitude. Steve and I became friends. He was going to join me as a guest on the Higher Purpose Podcast for episode 101 set to air on July 2, 2019, to ground the next 100 episodes in gratitude.

A couple of weeks before that date, I had an idea—what if we hosted a gratitude challenge and invited people to join us to explore the difference gratitude would make in their life. I called Steve and asked, "What do you think of us hosting a gratitude challenge?"

His immediate response, without asking the first question: "I'm in! Let's do it!"

Two weeks later, we launched our first 10-Day Gratitude Challenge. We have now hosted over 1,750 people from 50+ countries in the exploration of gratitude.

What do you offer?

I help companies tap into the power of purpose and see purpose transform their organizations. We work in areas of purpose, culture, and leadership serving companies that are purpose-driven, values-based, and people-focused.

Gratitude is now a part of all the work I do—formally or informally. I use gratitude as the opening for workshops or sessions to shift the atmosphere and create environments rich with possibility rather than rife with conflict.

I host a variety of Gratitude Challenges. Many of these are public and open to anyone interested in joining.

Gratitude Infusion

Increasingly, leaders of companies are asking me to help them incorporate gratitude into their culture and company. We now customize challenges for companies who want to incorporate gratitude into their values.

What have you gained by shifting your focus to gratitude?

WOW! What have I gained by shifting my focus to gratitude? Immense joy and amazing fulfillment. Partnerships and friendships with people from around the world. The JOY of introducing so many people to the life-changing and mind-altering practice of gratitude.

It's funny. As I said, I include gratitude in every session that I do—as an icebreaker or a foundational activity—regardless of what topic I'm actually addressing. And so often, when people are asked what were the big ideas they heard or main takeaways they have from the sessions...it's something about gratitude or the Abundance Loop.

It has even led to me being recognized or labeled as a "gratitude guru"—not a label I would ever apply to myself. I am happy to serve as a guide, but I am not a guru. I'm a work in progress.

To be honest, it was through the Gratitude Challenge that I met Kerry, became friends with her, and was asked to contribute to this book.

What difference has this made on your life?

More peace of mind—even in very tough times and difficult seasons of life and business.

What difference has this made on the lives of others?

That is the best part! "Transformational" is a word I hear often. The practice of gratitude transformed the way our team relates to one another. Incorporating gratitude into our meetings changes the atmosphere from that of griping and complaining to appreciation, celebration, and teamwork.

"Life-changing" is another word that comes up often during the Gratitude Challenges I host.

How would you suggest an individual get started with adding gratitude into their life?

Start small, start simple...and start NOW. Seriously! Pause right this moment and consider—what is something you are grateful for this very moment? And join us for the next Gratitude Challenge.

How would you suggest a company incorporate gratitude into their culture?

Lead by example! Go first! If you are the leader, start by sharing what you are grateful for. Maybe even do that for several meetings before you ever ask others what they are grateful for.

Write thank you notes. Make them personal, sincere, and handwritten.

Look for ways to incorporate gratitude into your existing meetings, tools, and resources. There are ways to do this that are high tech, low tech, and no tech.

High tech: Use an internal messaging system to spread messages of gratitude. My friends at TINY Pulse have a "cheers for peers" feature as part of their software where anybody in the organization can recognize any employee, customer, or even a supplier and share a cheer for them. Set up a gratitude channel on your Slack and have gratitude call-outs several times a day or week. Host a gratitude challenge inside your company. Need help? Partner with us to customize your own version of the Gratitude Challenge.

Low tech: Use a whiteboard in the break room or common area and list a gratitude prompt and allow people to post what they are grateful for.

No tech: Start every meeting by asking everyone to share ONE thing they are grateful for.

Contact:

www.thegratitudechallenge.community

Listen to the *Higher Purpose Podcast* on your favorite podcast player or by visiting higherpurposepodcast.com. And of course, connect with me personally. I'm active on LinkedIn and Twitter. Email me at kevin@kevindmonroe.com or call or text me at +1-404-713-0713... yes, that is my personal mobile number.

Name: Christel B. Wendelberger

Company: Mindful Gratitude

Personal Impact: I was introduced to Christel through Steve Foran who was very inspired by her book, *Mindful Gratitude: Practicing the Art of Appreciation*. I feel so grateful to have been connected to so many wonderful people with insightful testimonies on how gratitude has changed their lives.

What does gratitude mean to you?

Gratitude means deeper connection to the people, places, activities, and experiences of life. It's a ticket out of the doldrums and into a more meaningful interpretation of the human experience. Gratitude can heal and build relationships. It can be an antidote to sadness, loneliness, and stress. It can be a lifeline in our darkest hours. Gratitude is one of the most accessible, expansive, and practical gateways to emotional wellness, spiritual growth, and stronger interpersonal connections.

Gratitude is NOT a platitude. It's a life PRACTICE. It shouldn't be confused with "positive thinking" or dismissed as a superficial self-help balm. Gratitude is deep, and to reap its rich benefits, it must become an intentional practice; an investigation into and appreciation of the endless ways in which nature, human ingenuity, and individuals near and far support and bolster every aspect of our work and lives.

Why did you start the movement? Why did you include gratitude as a key component?

After nearly 25 years of organizational consulting in the areas of communication and philanthropy, I've seen dozens and dozens of workplace cultures, observed thousands of professional interactions, and watched leaders elevate and empower their teams as well as demean and demoralize them. Time and time again, I see that when people appreciate and respect the contributions of their colleagues, teams and projects flourish. When they don't, teams disintegrate and projects flounder and flop.

Successful leaders—whether they are CEOs, parents, teachers, salespeople, public servants, or anyone else seeking to make a positive impact on others—recognize the critical need to develop and strengthen key emotional intelligence skills. In our complex, ever-changing, 24/7 culture, skills like empathy, resilience, mindfulness, authentic listening, and positive communication are essential. Learning to pause, reflect, notice, and appreciate the contributions, circumstances, styles, and perceptions of others is essential to both personal well-being AND achieving successful organizational outcomes.

Research has proven that gratitude is one of the easiest entry points for helping people to "unhook" from stress, tap into their natural reservoirs of positive emotion, and reset their mood and approach to life's challenges. Through my book, workshops, presentations, and products, I want to help others develop and strengthen their natural capacity for gratitude. Ultimately, I hope I can help people to live their best lives, do their best work, and be the positive change we very much need in the world!

What do you offer?

We offer workshops, retreats, and keynote presentations focused on enhancing resiliency, reducing stress, strengthening relationships, and building more respectful, empathetic, and supportive cultures. Blending three research-based wellness principles—mindfulness, gratitude, and journaling—these experiential workshops and retreats offer participants opportunities to reflect and recharge as they practice new skills and experience the benefits in real time. The goal is for participants to experience such a positive shift that they are inspired to continue their practice of gratitude and organically transform the cultures of their organizations, families, and communities.

We also offer organizations the opportunity to showcase their commitment to wellness and positive culture with meaningful Mindful Gratitude gifts for employees, customers, vendors, and special events. In addition to the book *Mindful Gratitude: Practicing the Art of Appreciation*, we offer a line of journals, notecards, inspirational stickers, and T-shirts based on the gorgeous work of artist Timothy Meyerring.

What have you gained by shifting your focus to gratitude?

One of the greatest gifts my parents gave me was a capacity to be grateful, to see and celebrate the simple things, and to appreciate how other people contribute to my life. These lessons have allowed me to savor the best things in life AND weather the worst times. When sadness, illness, disappointment, loss, or conflict come along—and they always do in this life—my natural sense of gratitude provides a light in the darkness. Sometimes it's just a dim flicker, but I know to look for it.

What difference has this made on your life?

When my dear, dear dad was diagnosed with cancer and given nine months to live, I was also pregnant with our third child, running a full-time consulting business, and living on fumes. One early evening, after I collapsed on the couch in exhaustion and despair, I had a moment of quiet. An old friend had dropped off an amazing meal so I didn't have to cook. Another friend had taken the kids to their after-school activities. I sat and thought about how lucky I was to have those beautiful friends. I thought about how lucky I was to have clean running water and electricity that turned on like magic; a pantry full of food that I didn't have to grow; comfortable furniture, clothing, and a zillion other things that I did not have to make. It struck me that I was being supported in that very moment by the inventions, systems, and ingenuity of generations of humans. And in the midst of my loss, fear, and pain, I also had an overwhelming feeling of gratitude that balanced the suffering and gave me the hope I needed.

I decided to write *Mindful Gratitude: Practicing the Art of Appreciation* because I realized that my natural capacity for gratitude is a gift that was instilled in me, and I wanted to find a way to help others to both EXPERIENCE the depth and power of gratitude and LEARN how to practice and access it by reframing the stories of their own lives. Ultimately, I think the human story is one of connection. The more we can each see that, the more we will see each other and the more we can generate collaborative solutions to the challenges facing the world.

What difference has this made on the lives of others?

I've had the privilege of seeing firsthand the power and equalizing impact of the Mindful Gratitude experience on very diverse groups of people. From a team of emergency doctors who staff a Level I Trauma Center to a group of foster care social workers, from elected officials to road construction crews, from a 6th grade Girl Scout troop to a roomful of 80- and 90-year-olds, I have seen people connect with themselves and others through our process of reflection and expression of gratitude! Consistently, we hear things like, "This is the best team-building activity we've ever done." "This is the best training I've ever attended." "It changed my entire way of thinking." Here's how the Director of Resident Life at a large senior living community put it: "The Mindful Gratitude workshop was transformational for our residents. The guided exercises cultivated wonderful memories and created a spirit of joy and peace among participants."

How would you suggest an individual get started with adding gratitude into their life?

I think it all starts with a commitment to PRACTICING and to re-training your brain to intentionally LOOK for the good stuff. Our brains are wired to look for danger. This is an evolutionary survival mechanism. So we need to practice looking for the good stuff and saying THANK YOU for it!

Gratitude Infusion

My favorite practice is keeping a gratitude journal. Research demonstrates that writing down the good stuff can reduce clinical depression and anxiety as well as build our resiliency to confront the very real challenges that face us. You can write in the morning, the evening, throughout the day, or all of the above! If you start in the morning, jot down at least two things that are good in your life. This allows you to start your day centered in your own self-identified place of goodness. A bedtime gratitude journal helps you to review your day and identify and articulate the good things that you encountered. Even on a difficult day, intentionally recalling the good moments—a tasty snack, a laugh with a coworker, or a call from an old friend—allows you to reframe, unhook from worry, and balance out your perception of the day.

HINT: If you're feeling lonely, sad, or stuck, try listing the names of your favorite song, book, movie, or TV show and use a few words to describe what you love about them. Be grateful to the artists who opened their imaginations and created those wonderful things for you to enjoy!

Think about your favorite sweater, chair, or other comfort item. Write down what you love about them. Stop to think about the long chain of human connectivity that delivered them to you—from designer to factory workers to distributors and retailers—lots of human beings are responsible for bringing us most of our favorite things.

In addition to journaling, just start NOTICING your life more! Notice when a stranger holds a door for you, when your spouse takes out the recyclables or cooks a tasty meal, or when a clerk goes out of her way for you at the grocery store. Notice and SAY THANK YOU!

How would you suggest a company incorporate gratitude into their culture?

Just like incorporating gratitude into one's personal life, an organization needs to start by making an intentional commitment to a practice of gratitude. It helps tremendously when the commitment comes from the C-suite, but, of course, any individual can act as a leader and contribute to a grateful culture. The healthiest organizations are those that truly RESPECT the talents, contributions, and significance of every position and individual, and gratitude is one of the highest expressions of respect.

We offer consulting services to help organizations develop and implement meaningful gratitude practices, but those on a limited budget can certainly create them internally. Starting with a simple "Pause, Notice, Thank" policy is one easy way to begin. Pause, Notice, Thank can be designed in a variety of ways to fit the organization; it might include such things as managers taking time to write a public acknowledgement to at least one employee at least once a week. It might include starting or closing each meeting with a round of thank yous. It should always include signage, stickers, etc. that are around the workplace as reminders.

However an organization decides to express gratitude, it should always be SPECIFIC and MEANINGFUL. In other words, say thank you AND explain the specific impact the person's actions or contributions had on another individual, a team, a project, or the larger goals of the organization. We humans like to know that our actions have meaning, and when we understand our impact, we are motivated to do more! The important thing is for an organization to recognize the power of gratitude to build connections, inspire productivity, and increase employee wellness. Once that recognition is there, leaders need to make the commitment and make it happen.

What other easy infusions, in addition and similar to gratitude, would you suggest for improving Culture?

Again, I think it all boils down to respect and empathy—respect for the important role that each person plays in an organization and empathy for the circumstances and perspectives that influence individual behavior and outcomes. And again, setting the tone for respect, empathy, gratitude, and all of the elements that create a strong culture is the responsibility of those at the highest levels of leadership.

One easy practice that can be implemented by leaders at any level and which can dramatically impact outcomes is opening every meeting with a pause. Brendon Burchard, the world-renowned corporate coach and personal development expert, suggests that individuals regulate and reset their perspective every time they shift activities throughout the day. He suggests a practice of "Release Tension. Set Intention." The idea is that as you shift from one task to another, you intentionally release any tension or stress from the last activity and set a specific intention for the new one. This same approach can transform the meeting experience. If at the start of each meeting, the leader offers one minute of complete silence and asks the group to internally release tension and set their own intention for a positive meeting, imagine how much more centered, efficient, and productive participants can be!

Contact:

To connect with us, visit www.mindfulgratitude.com, where you can sign up for our informational e-newsletter, purchase books and products, and get more information about how to schedule your Mindful Gratitude workshop, retreat, or consultation. You can also like Mindful Gratitude on Facebook and follow us on Instagram.

GRATITUDE-EXPANDING EXPERIENCES

Personal: Try answering the same questions that each case study participant did. Do you have any insights on gratitude to share?

Workplace: Reflect on how you can bring any of the above ideas from the case studies to life in your career.

Gratitude Infusion: What is one small change you can make today at home or in the workplace to be more grateful?

CHAPTER 12

Conclusion

As we come to the end of the book, I hope that you are inspired to infuse gratitude into your personal and professional lives. As I shared in the introduction, a wise soul said, "No matter the language gratitude is given in, it's always understood, appreciated, and never forgotten."

Gratitude is always the answer. While it may take practice to train yourself to view life from a glass-half-full perspective, it will be well worth it as you begin to recognize all your blessings. We can connect with others on a deeper level when we focus on the good, and we open our hearts to love and understanding. When we practice gratitude daily, it no longer becomes a thing we must put effort into doing. When life is good, we are grateful. When life is bad or uncertain, we are grateful. It helps make the good moments great and the bad moments more palatable.

After reading about how gratitude has changed my life and the lives of others, I now pass the torch onto you. How can you be a role model of gratitude in your workplace and personal relationships?

We've covered a lot of strategies in this book that you could use. For example:

- Recognize how others receive gratitude and customize your gratitude for each receiver

- Be generous and specific when you give others gratitude

- Use gratitude when facing challenges

- Get creative and use gratitude in how you reward your teams

- Explore how you can give back to others to complete the circle of gratitude

- Expand your network of like-minded people

Together, let's spread and infuse gratitude daily to lift each other's spirits and recognize our unique gifts. Each one of us has the opportunity to lead by example by choosing to live in gratitude. As you make notice of being grateful in your life, be sure to share with others so that they may follow your example. Gratitude is meant to be shared.

CHAPTER 13

Outward Gratitude

A book on gratitude shall end in an outward expression of gratitude. The individuals below helped inspire this book or contributed to enabling the message to flow. I am grateful to:

My team at Actualize for reviewing, offering enhancements, and editing, including Maddie Yaskowski, Valentina Dragolova, Lori Lite, and Theresa Santoro.

My editors who agreed to help with another book. I was thrilled to have the support of Heidi King and Amy Scott.

My kiddos, Audrey and Blaine, as without their zest for life, I would not have such a fresh perspective.

Joe Burnham for talking through the gratitude bubble concept.

Jackie Smith for the cover and inside cover designs and graphics in the book. We have worked together as long as I have needed a graphic artist, and I cherish how she magically portrays my vision.

The Actualize Partners, Chad Wekelo and Matt Seu, for your continued openness, belief, and support in our people first at Actualize.

To those who contributed case studies and allowed me to use your stories, thank you. The book is much richer with your experiences.

NOTES

1. Emmons, R. A. (2013). *Gratitude Works! A Twenty-One Day Program for Creating Emotional Prosperity.* San Francisco: Jossey-Bass.

2. Wekelo, K. A. (2017). *Culture Infusion: 9 Principles to Create and Maintain a Thriving Organizational Culture.* Peaceful Daily, Inc.

3. Wekelo, K. A. (2017). *Wonders of Your Mind.* Peaceful Daily, Inc.

4. See more about my daily principles at http://www.zen-doway.com/principles1.html.

5. Fox, G. (2017, August 4). "What Can the Brain Reveal about Gratitude?" *Greater Good Magazine.* https://greatergood.berkeley.edu/article/item/what_can_the_brain_reveal_about_gratitude.

6. Emmons, R. A., and M. E. McCullough. (2004). *The Psychology of Gratitude.* New York: Oxford University Press.

7. Gostick, A. R., and C. Elton. (2020). *Leading with Gratitude: Eight Leadership Practices for Extraordinary Business Results.* New York: Harper Business.

8. Restrepo, Sandra, dir. (2019). *Brené Brown: The Call to Courage*. Netflix Special.

9. Brown, B. (2018, November 21). "Brené Brown on Joy and Gratitude." Global Leadership Network. https://global-leadership.org/articles/leading-yourself/brene-brown-on-joy-and-gratitude/.

10. Gibran, Kahlil. (1952). *The Prophet*. New York: Knopf.

11. Emmons, R. A. (2016). *The Little Book of Gratitude: Create a Life of Happiness and Well Being by Giving Thanks*. London: Gaia Books Ltd.

12. Learn more about Actualize's Moving with Gratitude Challenge at https://www.youtube.com/watch?v=PB26MQ7ZYwk&t=.

13. Check out my Gratitude Cube at http://www.zendoway.com/gratitude.html.

14. Allen, S. (2018, May 10). "Why Is Gratitude So Hard for Some People?" *Greater Good Magazine*. https://greatergood.berkeley.edu/article/item/why_is_gratitude_so_hard_for_some_people.

15. Wong, J., and J. Brown. (2017, June 6). "How Gratitude Changes You and Your Brain." *Greater Good Magazine*. https://greatergood.berkeley.edu/article/item/how_gratitude_changes_you_and_your_brain.

16. Beck, M. (n.d.). "Receive with an Open Heart: Giving and Accepting Gifts of Real Love." *Martha's Blog*. https://marthabeck.com/2012/08/receiving-open-heart/.

17. Wekelo, K. A. (2017). *Culture Infusion: 9 Principles to Create and Maintain a Thriving Organizational Culture.* Peaceful Daily, Inc.

18. Emmons, R. A. (2013). *Gratitude Works! A Twenty-One Day Program for Creating Emotional Prosperity.* San Francisco: Jossey-Bass.

19. Emmons, R. A. (2013, May 13). "How Gratitude Can Help You Through Hard Times." *Greater Good Magazine.* https://greatergood.berkeley.edu/article/item/how_gratitude_can_help_you_through_hard_times.

20. Hanh, T. N. (2010). *A Pebble for Your Pocket: Mindful Stories for Children and Grown-Ups.* Berkeley, CA: Plum Blossom Books.

21. Hanh, T. N. (2013). *The Art of Communicating.* New York: Harper One.

22. Check out my Feelings Cube at http://www.zendoway.com/feelings.html.

23. Emmons, R. A. (2016). *The Little Book of Gratitude: Create a Life of Happiness and Well Being by Giving Thanks.* London: Gaia Books Ltd.

24. Wekelo, K. A. (2017). *Culture Infusion: 9 Principles to Create and Maintain a Thriving Organizational Culture.* Peaceful Daily, Inc.

25. Check out our Intentional Acts of Kindness Challenge at https://www.youtube.com/watch?v=FJRHbNSolrY&t=1s.

26. Yaskowski, M. (n.d.). "Giving Back Through Wellness." *Corporate Wellness Magazine.* https://www.corporatewellnessmagazine.com/article/giving-back-wellness.

27. Wekelo, K. A., & M. Yaskowski. (n.d.). "3 Reasons for Hands-On Giving." *Corporate Wellness Magazine.* https://www.corporatewellnessmagazine.com/article/3-reasons-hands-giving.

CPSIA information can be obtained
at www.ICGtesting.com
Printed in the USA
BVHW081146220620
582039BV00002BA/175